GEORGES FEYDEAU

WORLD DRAMATISTS
In the same series:

Edward Albee	*Ronald Hayman*
Samuel Beckett	*Ronald Hayman*
Calderón	*Heinz Gerstinger*
·Anton Chekhov	*Siegfried Melchinger*
Euripides	*Siegfried Melchinger*
Georges Feydeau	*Leonard C. Pronko*
Carlo Goldoni	*Heinz Riedt*
Henrik Ibsen	*Hans Georg Meyer*
Christopher Marlowe	*Gerald Pinciss*
Arthur Miller	*Ronald Hayman*
John Osborne	*Ronald Hayman*
Harold Pinter	*Ronald Hayman*
Luigi Pirandello	*Renate Matthaei*
Arthur Schnitzler	*Reinhard Urbach*
Sophocles	*Siegfried Melchinger*
August Strindberg	*Gunnar Ollén*
Lope de Vega and Spanish Drama	*Heinz Gerstinger*
Arnold Wesker	*Ronald Hayman*

GEORGES

FEYDEAU

LEONARD C. PRONKO

WITH HALFTONE ILLUSTRATIONS

FREDERICK UNGAR PUBLISHING CO.
NEW YORK

Copyright © 1975 by Frederick Ungar Publishing Co., Inc.
Printed in the United States of America
Library of Congress Catalog Card Number: 74-16788
Designed by Edith Fowler
ISBN: 0-8044-2700-3

6/84

CONTENTS

Chronology   1
Georges Feydeau and La Belle Epoque   5
The Geometry of Madness   21
The Taste for Truth   52
The Plays   76
       Tailleur pour dames   76
       Monsieur chasse   91
       Champignol malgré lui   101
       Un Fil à la patte   109
       L'Hôtel du Libre-Echange   116
       Le Dindon   123
       La Dame de chez Maxim   132
       La Main passe   145
       Le Bourgeon   152
       La Puce à l'oreille   157
       Occupe-toi d'Amélie   166
       Feu la mère de madame   175
       On purge bébé   179
       "Mais n'te promène donc pas toute
          nue!"   182
       Léonie est en avance   185
       Hortense a dit: "Je m'en fous!" 188
Conclusion: The Moral of the Tale   191
Notes   201
Bibliography   205
Index   210

CHRONOLOGY

1862   Georges Feydeau born, December 8, in Paris, son of Ernest Feydeau, a well-known writer and scholar. His mother was a fabulously beautiful Polish woman, Lodzia Zelewska. It was rumored that the child's true father was either the Duke of Morny or Napoleon III.

1883   First professional production, *Amour et piano* (Love and Piano),* 1 act, at the Athénée. A *succès d'estime*.

1884   Feydeau recommends Henri Becque's *La Parisienne* (*Woman of Paris*), destined to become one of the masterpieces of naturalist theatre, for production at the Renaissance, where he is secretary to the manager.

1886   Feydeau's first great theatrical success, *Tailleur pour dames* (*A Gown for His Mistress*),* 3 acts, at the Renaissance. The works written in the following seven years failed to live up to the promise of this comedy.

1889   Feydeau marries the wealthy and beautiful

* To aid the reader, published translations are distinguished from literal translations by the use of italics.

daughter of the famous portrait painter Carolus-Duran, and he momentarily solves his pecuniary difficulties.

1892   Beginning of the major works: *Monsieur chasse* (*The Happy Hunter*), 3 acts, at the Palais-Royal, and *Champignol malgré lui* (Champignol in Spite of Himself), 3 acts, in collaboration with Maurice Desvallières, at the Nouveautés.

1894   *Un Fil à la patte* (*Cat Among Pigeons* or *Not by Bed Alone*), 3 acts, at the Palais-Royal. *L'Hôtel du Libre-Echange* (*Hotel Paradiso*), 3 acts, in collaboration with Maurice Desvallières, at the Nouveautés. *Le Ruban* (The Decoration), a comedy of character, at the Odéon, a government subsidized theater second only to the Comédie-Française.

1896   *Le Dindon* (The Dupe), 3 acts, at the Palais-Royal.

1899   Feydeau's greatest success during his lifetime, *La Dame de chez Maxim* (*The Lady from Maxim's*), 3 acts, at the Nouveautés. Feydeau discovers Armande Cassive for the role of la Môme Crevette, and molds her into the perfect interpreter for his major female roles.

1904   *La Main passe* (*Chemin de fer*), 4 acts, at the Nouveautés.

1906   *Le Bourgeon* (The Sprout), 3 acts, at the Vaudeville. Feydeau's only "serious" play.

1907   *La Puce à l'oreille* (*A Flea in Her Ear*), 3 acts, at the Nouveautés. Feydeau's most popular play in English-speaking countries.

1908   *Occupe-toi d'Amélie* (*Keep an Eye on Amélie* or *Look After Lulu*), 3 acts at the Nouveautés.

Feu la mère de madame (*Madam's Late Mother*), 1 act, at the Comédie-Royale; the first of Feydeau's short, bitterly misogynic plays which he intended to publish together under the general title *From Marriage to Divorce*.

1909 Following a particularly violent domestic quarrel, Feydeau leaves his home, moving to the Hotel Terminus where, for almost ten years, he will live among piles of books, surrounded by his collection of famous paintings and his equally beloved collection of some 250 perfumes.

On purge bébé (*Going to Pot*), 1 act, at the Nouveautés.

1911 *"Mais n'te promène donc pas toute nue!"* ("Don't Walk Around Stark Naked!"), 1 act, at the Fémina. *Léonie est en avance, ou Le Mal joli* (*Léonie is Ahead of Time*), 1 act, at the Comédie-Royale.

1914 *Je ne trompe pas mon mari* (I'm Not Deceiving My Husband), 3 acts, in collaboration with René Peter, at the Athénée. Feydeau's final full-length play.

1916 *Hortense a dit: "Je m'en fous!"* (Hortense Said: "I don't give a damn!"), 1 act, at the Palais-Royal. Feydeau's last play.

1919 Feydeau moves to a sanatorium where he can be treated for neurasthenia. During his last years he is only intermittently lucid.

1921 Feydeau dies.

1941 *Feu la mère de madame* enters the repertory of the Comédie-Française as a curtain-raiser.

1948 The revival of *Occupe-toi d'Amélie* by Jean-

Louis Barrault and Madeleine Renaud at the Marigny marks the beginning of Feydeau's immense postwar popularity.

1951 *Le Dindon*, soon to be followed by other full-length plays, enters the repertory of the Comédie-Française, thereby consecrating Feydeau as a modern "classic."

GEORGES FEYDEAU AND
LA BELLE EPOQUE

More than any other French writer of the turn of the century, Georges Feydeau typifies that period of gaiety, optimism and high living known as *la belle époque*. While no single author can represent an entire epoch, his complicated dramatic constructions evoke the atmosphere associated with the happy "good old days" when the well-to-do bourgeois believed that things were for the best in a world which allowed him to devote his leisure (and almost all his time was leisure) to the pursuit of pleasure. Lurking beneath the frenetically joyous surface, however, is a vision of the world in explosion which was to go almost unnoticed until the midyears of the twentieth century—a vision which gives depth and bite to comedies and farces which might otherwise have perished with the halcyon days they depict. If that vision tempts us to describe Feydeau's world as "the underside of the *belle époque*," such a tag is justified as well by the number of scenes in which characters appear in various states of undress.

For Feydeau is king of the bedroom farce and brought that much denigrated form to its height of perfection before it fell into the vulgarity and dullness of its current doldrums.

Marcel Achard, a reigning dramatist of the Paris boulevard theater, has called Feydeau the greatest French comic writer after Molière.[1] Like his great predecessor, Feydeau was a melancholy man, perhaps because the year of his birth, 1862, also marked the publication of his scholarly father's *History of Burial Customs and Graves Among the Ancients*. But his father was a novelist as well and bequeathed to his son his literary leanings. Ernest Feydeau's best-known work, *Fanny*, was apparently so licentious that it was denounced from his pulpit by the Archbishop of Paris. The resulting heavy sales inspired the author to dedicate the following edition to "the Archbishop of Paris in grateful acknowledgment."

Young Georges was first exposed to the theater as a child of six or seven, and returned home so overwhelmed that he set to work on his own play almost immediately. His father, impressed by the boy's diligence, urged his governess not to bother him with studies that day, since he had already written a play. Georges saw here a method of sidestepping his studies whenever he had failed to prepare his homework, and he whimsically claimed that it was his laziness that led him to the theater. In later years the successful dramatist would say that he detested writing now that it had become his profession, and that he much preferred to spend his time painting.

The quiet, rather elegant laziness of Feydeau has become legendary, and many stories are told reflecting his reluctance to exert himself. "Look at that magnificent woman!" urged a friend one day while the two were seated in a cafe. "Where is she?" asked Feydeau. "Behind you." "Oh, describe her to me."[2]

Conscious of his laziness, Feydeau once dismissed the attentions of a cloakroom attendant helping him on with his coat: "Don't bother. This is my only form of exercise."[3]

The young playwright's first theatrical attempts were in salon comedies, short scenes and monologues, performed at social gatherings, sometimes by Feydeau himself, who had no mean talent as an actor. At one time he almost gave up writing to become an actor. He had lost all his money gambling (and was later to lose millions of francs on the stock market), and to make the money to pay his gas bill he was ready to sign a contract as an actor at the Théâtre du Vaudeville. When a friend lent him the necessary money, Feydeau went off to gamble again, won this time, and was able to pay his bill and keep on gambling. The manager of the Vaudeville had in the meantime hired another actor, and Feydeau met the lovely and wealthy young woman who was to become his wife and save, for a time, his pecuniary position.[4]

Feydeau's first professionally staged play was a short work, *Amour et piano* (1883; Love and Piano)* which is based upon the *quiproquo*—or mistaken identity—which plays such an important role in nineteenth-century farce and vaudeville. It reveals the author's indebtedness to his predecessors, and gives a foretaste of the sense of the absurd which was to flourish in his later masterpieces.

* English translations are supplied for all of Feydeau's plays; a title in italics indicates a published English version.

Edouard, a handsome wealthy young provincial just recently come to Paris, has decided to look up, sight unseen, the popular actress Dubarroy, in hopes of becoming her lover. This, he feels, will establish him as an elegant man about town. He makes a mistake in the number of the house and is introduced into the salon of Lucile's apartment, where the innocent young girl is awaiting the arrival of her new piano teacher. Using many asides, each comments upon the strange behavior of his or her interlocutor, and Feydeau plays upon the various comic possibilities of the situation, reaching a climax when Edouard, having been asked to beat time while Lucile plays the piano, thinks he has been asked to beat the furniture, and raises clouds of dust. Only in the last minutes of the play do the young people realize their mistake, and they part hoping that they may soon be properly introduced.

Although much simpler than geometrical triumphs like *La Puce à l'oreille* (*A Flea in Her Ear*) or *L'Hôtel du Libre-Echange* (*Hotel Paradiso*), *Amour et piano* shows the skillful mingling of the comedy of words (including foreign words) and the violent physical comedy of farce, with the dominant comedy of situation. Love, marriage, and the demimonde announce Feydeau's major themes, and the idle milieu of wealthy ladies and men about town with nothing better to do than devote themselves to the pursuit of love and sex, sets the scene for the works yet to come.

Feydeau's first popular success and his first long play was *Tailleur pour dames* (1886; *A Gown for His Mistress*). This triumph raised his hopes, which were sadly disappointed by the failures or half-successes of his next seven plays, four of them in collaboration with

Maurice Desvallières. Finally, in 1890, Feydeau decided to stop writing for a time in order to study the writers who had succeeded in the farce and vaudeville: Eugène Labiche for his sense of observation, Henri Meilhac for his dialogue, and Alfred Hennequin, the master of French vaudeville, for his dramatic construction.

Profiting from this contact with the masters of his genre, by 1892 he produced two new plays, *Monsieur chasse* (*The Happy Hunter*) and *Champignol malgré lui* (Champignol in Spite of Himself), the latter again in collaboration with Desvallières. He submitted both to the manager of the Palais-Royal, who was delighted to accept *Monsieur chasse*, but advised the young author to put *Champignol* away forever—it was so inept that it could never succeed. Happy to have one play accepted, Feydeau went on his way, and in front of the Nouveautés encountered Micheau, the manager of that theater which had recently produced a series of failures and was about to close its doors. Micheau asked to see the manuscript Feydeau was carrying, and after much resistance from the author, who was convinced *Champignol* was too absurd to produce, the desperate manager finally received the text. He read it immediately and decided on the spot to produce it. Ironically, it proved a far greater success than *Monsieur chasse*.

Champignol malgré lui opened a period of uninterrupted successes for Feydeau. For the next sixteen years, every year or two a new play appeared, bringing high praise from the critics and hysterical laughter from the audiences. Until 1908 and after, Feydeau was the most popular author of the boulevard theater; his plays were performed abroad almost as frequently as in Paris, and sometimes translated into many foreign languages before they had yet been performed in France.

Despite his success, Feydeau was not a happy man. Little is known of his personal life, but it is surmised that his marriage was not particularly felicitous. It is not difficult to imagine the loneliness of Marianne Feydeau while her husband, rarely at home, pursued his nocturnal life with actors, writers and the demimonde. If we assume that the picture of married life which emerges from his plays reflects his own marriage, then life at home must have become intolerable some time during the first decade of the new century. The wife depicted in the final five short plays (1908–1916) —and she is essentially the same woman, no matter what her name—is a vixen of the worst sort, persecuting her ineffectual husband almost to the point of madness. Feydeau had intended to gather these plays, all comedies of character rather than farce, into a collection entitled, "From Marriage to Divorce," but he never did so—perhaps because the divorce actually took place in his own life in 1916.

In September, 1909, after a particularly violent quarrel with Mme Feydeau, the author moved out of his home and took up residence in the Hotel Terminus, near the Gare St. Lazare. He remained there for almost ten years, surrounding himself with the paintings and perfumes he loved, and working less and less. His melancholia turned blacker, and finally his unsettled mental state required that he be moved to a sanatorium. He died there in 1921, never having regained full sanity, and sometimes even believing himself to be Napoleon III.

The portrait of Feydeau which constantly recurs is

that of a melancholy man of great refinement and personal beauty, seated midst crowds in a lively cafe, listening silently, observing life about him through half-closed eyes that were screened by the rising smoke of his ever-present cigar. Reserved and aristocratic, cold to some, to most he was gracious, gentle and natural. His friend, Robert de Flers, another successful writer of comedies, describes him thus:

> Through his cigar smoke he observed mankind, if I may say so, with a kind of attentive distraction. He dreamed endlessly. But since the stars seemed too far to him, and the moonlight too pale and the ideal a bit worn thin, he dreamed of life, and that is why he only smiled faintly. This great concocter of joys was a melancholic. At the same time, and quite naturally, he enjoyed being a living, charming paradox. He was infinitely cordial with a bit of coolness, very sensitive beneath apparent indifference, ambitious with modesty, nonchalantly hardworking, and sadly good-humored.[6]

When he spoke, it was often to deliver a witty sally which quickly went the rounds of Paris society. Usually they were cruelly critical and revealed that he had not wasted his time when he spent hours observing the frantic life going on about him. But even the cruelty was lightened by the complete naturalness with which the comment was proffered. Of an acquaintance whom friends had declared was good for nothing but being cuckolded, Feydeau declared, "Yes, and even there he needs his wife to help him."

Asked by an actor whether he had seen his recent performance, the dramatist replied, "But, of course, I did, my friend. And I hope you'll forgive me."

This sad and taciturn writer of the gayest comedies of our century, confided to his friends, "Life is short, but we get bored all the same." In his escape from boredom, Feydeau lived the life of the true *fin de siècle* boulevardier. From early evening to early morning he could be found in the cafes and restaurants of that fashionable part of *belle époque* Paris, the *grands boulevards*, newly pierced through the heart of Second Empire Paris under the direction of Baron Haussmann. Since 1880 they have formed the main arteries of the right bank. At the time Feydeau flourished they were the site of stylish shops, popular music halls known then as *café-concerts*, and expensive restaurants and cafes, each catering to a particular clientele. The two most frequented by Feydeau were the Napolitain and Maxim's.

The Napolitain was the headquarters for journalists, poets and other *littérateurs* and men of wit. Somewhat bohemian, it knew moments of upset and even of violence. Indeed, it was here that the master duelers of Paris held out, and it was they that the offended and the offending were expected to consult in setting up the details of the frequent duels which took place. It was also here that Laurent Tailhade, spokesman for anarchy, ironically lost an eye in the explosion of a bomb thrown by an anarchist. But chiefly the Napolitain was frequented by men like Georges Courteline, Catulle Mendès and Toulouse-Lautrec. Every evening, between six and eight, just after rising, Feydeau would sit for an hour or so with his cigar in this noisy cafe. For supper he would go round the corner to Maxim's, passing on his way the fashionable Café Weber, haunt of the intellectual bourgeoisie, restaurant favored by Proust who showed up nightly just before midnight invariably to order his port and a bunch of grapes.

Maxim's, most famous of all the *belle époque* restaurants, immortalized in the title of Feydeau's most popular play, *La Dame de chez Maxim* (1899; *The Lady from Maxim's*), was the stronghold of fast livers, men of the world and ladies of easy virtue. It was here that wealthy men invariably spent the wee hours of the morning, and here that visiting royalty, princes, grand dukes and millionaires, came to wine and dine and entertain the most sought after—and the most expensive —courtesans of the day. Indeed, Maxim's stands as a kind of symbol of the fast, gay, easy-going life of the *belle époque*, for midst its stylish art nouveau décor, could be found entertainment, sexual titillation, sumptuous food in a variety and quantity that would stagger the vastest stomachs today, and forgetfulness of any disagreeable realities of the world outside.

It was here, no doubt, that Feydeau observed much of the life that appears with a startling, if obsessed, veracity in his plays. Here that he understood the fundamental egotism of men who live only for sensual pleasure, and the women who exist only to profit from that need. There are two major facets to Feydeau's picture of life: one is that of the bourgeois household, but the other is that of the demimonde, and even when we are within the confines of a well-regulated middle-class home, the threat offered by the attractive women of the half-world is always present.

From our vantage point in the twentieth century, it is difficult to understand the power and influence exercised by the kept women of the ending nineteenth and beginning twentieth centuries. Often coming from humble circumstances, and making their first public appearances as music-hall singers or dancers, or as circus entertainers, these women sometimes rose to dizzying heights. The "three greats" lived, at least for public view, the lives of great ladies of the aristocracy. Although they passed from hand to hand, or bed to bed, they were protected by grand dukes, crown princes, and princes, presented with fabulous diamonds, rubies and emeralds which had belonged to the crowned heads of Europe.

La Belle Otero, a Spanish dancer who earned from Americans the name of "the suicidal siren," whose fierce love of gambling ruined a number of her wealthy lovers, decided one evening to shame her rival, the refined Liane de Pougy, by appearing at Maxim's laden with all her jewels: a pearl necklace of the Empress Eugénie, a diamond necklace of Marie Antoinette, a necklace of the Empress of Austria, eight bracelets of rubies, emeralds, sapphires, a crown of brilliants, earrings of 50-carat diamonds each, and numerous smaller pieces. Liane de Pougy, who got wind of it, appeared in a startling white décolleté, wearing not a single piece of jewelry, but followed at a respectful distance by her chambermaid carrying a staggering weight of gems on a velvet cushion.

Although decent women would not have been caught at Maxim's, and young girls were stringently isolated from such tasty pictures of life, the distinctions between *le monde*, or good society, and *le demimonde*—which had already begun to break down in the middle of the nineteenth century—had become quite fuzzy by 1890. The family, center of the bourgeois sense of comfort and stability in 1850, was seriously attacked by the new divorce law promulgated in 1884. Time and again characters in Feydeau's plays threaten to divorce, or at any rate, they hold that possibility in reserve—as does the innocent young Viviane in *Un Fil à la patte* (1894; *Cat Among the Pigeons* or *Not By Bed Alone*). Even as she signs her marriage contract she remarks that, after all, if her husband doesn't please her, she can always get a divorce. Life, not to be outdone by art, furnished proof of Feydeau's veracity the following year: on the eve of the "marriage of the century," which took place in 1895 between the handsome young Parisian dandy Count Boni de Castellane and the fabulously wealthy but extremely plain American heiress Anna Gould, the bride had refused to embrace Catholicism, saying "It's too difficult to get a divorce when one is Catholic. I want to be able to divorce, if I'm unhappy with you."[6]

The *cocottes* of the *belle époque* (or *horizontales*, as they were more vulgarly called) enjoyed a certain status, and not only because they were kept by such men as Edward VII of England and William II of Germany. They were listed as well with the Ministry of Foreign Affairs, so that visiting dignitaries might find in Paris all the pleasures to which they were accustomed at home—and more. Claiming the standard excuse of an appointment with the President of the Senate, dignitaries were able to attend a rendezvous of a more personal nature. The status and social acceptance of the *cocottes* were further reflected in the newspaper columns which detailed the ladies' vicissitudes as they changed protectors, acquired jewels, or bedecked themselves in the latest fashions.

It was in this world that Feydeau spent his evenings, leaving only when his friends departed at three or four in the morning. As though he feared the moment he would be alone, he would accompany each one to his home, and then finally go back to the Hotel Terminus. Reluctant yet to sleep, he would spend long hours talking with the night porter or with the newspaper vendor at the all-night stand before the Gare St. Lazare.

Playwright Louis Verneuil (who, long after Feydeau's death, met the dramatist's daughter and married her), recounts how one morning in 1914 he was returning home about five o'clock when he stopped to purchase a newspaper at the kiosk in front of the Gare St. Lazare. What was his surprise to find Feydeau, seated on a chair before the kiosk, selling the newspapers. The writer explained that he was taking the vendor's place while she went to get a bowl of hot soup, and he invited Verneuil to sit and chat. He spent till 6:30 in lively conversation with his future son-in-law and the newspaper vendor.

Such pictures of Feydeau help balance the portrait of the somewhat distant aristocratic man or the stylish boulevardier frequenting the most talked about spots in town. They help us to understand how Feydeau the keen observer was able to reflect with the accent of truth not only the upper levels of society which he knew so well, but the life of servants, peasants and working people—each speaking his own language. The early morning Feydeau, conversing with a porter or newsvendor, provides a striking contrast to the brilliant playwright or the *bon vivant*, and suggests a lonely, haunted man, unwilling perhaps to face some frightening reality forced upon him when alone. Whatever the truth, we shall never know it, and Feydeau remains a tantalizingly enigmatic personality.

Like the brilliantly witty yet melancholy dramatist,

the *belle époque* has its dazzling obverse and its not so pleasant reverse. Paris, at the turn of the century, was the intellectual and artistic center of the western world. And just to prove it, the French staged a Universal Exposition there in 1900, following closely upon the heels of the lesser one in 1889 which had seen the erection of the Eiffel Tower. Life bubbled and glittered on the boulevards and in the crowded terraces of lively cafes and restaurants. The music hall, the circus, the dance halls of Montmartre, thrived. The well-to-do bourgeois of the infant Third Republic knew that life was good and that it was bound to last.

Not only had positivism and science promised a bright future offering a solution to many of man's problems, but *fin de siècle* man was witnessing a revolution that was to be as long-lasting in its results, though not so dramatically upsetting, as the one a hundred years earlier. Electricity was lighting up the capital and making it truly the City of Light, automobiles were seen on the streets, and by 1906 the first autobuses began to replace horse-drawn omnibuses. The distance from one end of Paris to the other was shortened by the installation of the new Métro, whose first line opened in 1900. Men were even learning to fly, and in 1909 Louis Blériot made the first crossing of the channel by air, while down on the ground Nijinsky was dazzling the eyes of Parisians by his incredible leaps in the Ballet Russe, presentations that conquered Paris and revealed new possibilities in theater and dance.

New, too, were the radium isolated by the Curies, the presence of x-rays and of heretofore unknown vitamins, the Cubist paintings of Braque and Picasso, the wildness of raw color in works of Matisse, Vlaminck and Derain, the cakewalk which caused a furor and found reflection in the music of Debussy, who was at the same time scandalizing the conservatives by his "formless" music for *Pelléas et Mélisande*.

Strictly speaking, the *belle époque* begins in 1900 and ends in 1910, but its spirit invades the years before and after. It was a period of happy forgetfulness, after the shameful French defeat at the hands of the Germans in the Franco-Prussian war of 1870, and a continuation of the gay days of the Second Empire when Haussmann first began the reconstruction of a new Paris to the tunes of Offenbach's irrepressible *Gaîté parisienne*, which seemed to sum up the spirit of the times.

It was a day of relaxed morals, huge meals, and a dramatic attitude toward life which saw everything as spectacle. It was the day of realism and naturalism on the one hand, and of the startling triumph of *Cyrano* on the other, revealing to the French a hope for dramatic poetry and what they liked to think of as the "French spirit," as opposed to the murky clouds of Symbolism and the northern mists of Ibsen and Strindberg. These are the years of *The Afternoon of a Faun*, of Jarry's truculent satire of the dominant bourgeois spirit, *Ubu roi*, of Sarah Bernhardt and Mounet-Sully, of Bergson's major philosophical writings, of Colette, Gide, Proust, Claudel, Apollinaire, Péguy. Years of richness and plenty in the arts, in the intellectual realms, and in the purses of the middle class.

They are also the years of the Panama scandal, when the French discovered corruption in high offices and lost a measure of faith in their republic; of the Dreyfus affair which brought to a head the struggle between the military and the intellectuals, revealed a strong vein of antisemitism, and ended, after distressing and tragic events, with the vindication of a man broken by years of imprisonment on Devil's Island, and with a loss of face for the military. The underside of the *belle époque* reveals corruption, lawlessness, anarchy: bandits and bank robbers, the cruel world of Parisian lowlife, bombs exploding in the Chamber of Deputies, heads of state assassinated at the rate of almost one a year. There are, of course, the more juicy scandals of the day as well: the President of the Republic, Félix Faure, expiring of a heart attack in the arms of his mistress (while not far away, Feydeau's *La Dame de chez Maxim* celebrated similar pleasures with less dire results), the theft of the Mona Lisa from the Louvre in which the poet Apollinaire was freakishly implicated, the assassination of the managing editor of *Le Figaro* by Mme Caillaux, wife of a deputy, whose corruption the paper had exposed. But these morsels seem to belong somehow to the same theatrical world as the *cocottes*, the circus and the great cafes. The unrest and dissatisfaction reflected by widespread violence, anarchy and the frequency of strikes (even if for an apparently frivolous reason, as when the waiters of Paris struck for the right to wear moustaches) point to a fundamental instability which, even while the thoughtless *bon vivant* was drinking his absinthe or dallying with his *horizontale*, was threatening the equilibrium of that beautiful world he thought (or perhaps only desperately hoped) would never come to an end.

In 1914 it exploded with a vengeance. After World War I, the world of the *belle époque* seemed further away than the *ancien régime*, for it was based upon an optimism and self-satisfaction no longer possible after the years of cataclysm. The vaudevilles of Feydeau, written for the smug middle class whose egotism and naïveté they so clearly reflected, might well have passed into oblivion if they had done no more than that. For they are indeed the dazzling mirror of a frivolous and pleasure-seeking class which found itself so self-sufficient and interesting that it little cared to investigate what lay beyond its own limited world.

But Feydeau was able to suggest, below the ebullient surface, the threatening nightmare world beyond man's control, or even his comprehension. If his contemporaries were unaware of that dimension, that simply means that they were too preoccupied with the other pleasures offered by the most hilarious situations concocted by human imagination. The new sensibility fostered by the war and its aftermath, and even more the attitudes developed up to and through World War II, reflected in such important movements as Existentialism and the Theater of the Absurd, made spectators in the second half of the twentieth century aware of the contemporaneity of these apparently fluffy farces.

It is difficult, in the 1970s, to overlook the obvious affinities between our not so "belle" epoch, and the one we have just glanced at: easy morals, living for present pleasure, scandal in high places, failing confidence in government, discrediting of the military, and anarchy, bombs, and violence. There is certainly lacking in our day the brio and style of the *belle époque*—almost as though the underside of that earlier day had become the upper side of ours.

Feydeau's popularity today no doubt owes a good deal to these affinities, as it does to our nostalgia for the good old days and the carefree world they symbolize. But there is another important reason: we have not lost our taste for laughter. And Feydeau was an absolute master in creating that commodity.

THE GEOMETRY OF MADNESS

In the boulevard theater of the *belle époque*, Feydeau is a giant among pygmies. His personal genius, which ultimately drove him to madness, allowed him to create the complex dramatic structures which seem to whirl at such speed that they too threaten to fall over the brink into the abyss of lunacy. It is this very excess that is responsible for Feydeau's greatness, allowing him to suggest, through an apparently trivial subject, perceptions of a nightmare existence which are all too familiar to man in the last quarter of the twentieth century. Yet, like some perfect gyroscope, they remain miraculously balanced over the void, never quite toppling.

Like every dramatist writing for the bourgeois audiences of the boulevard theater, Feydeau fell heir to the formula of the well-made play. One would be tempted to qualify that formula as already outworn in the 1880s if it had not continued to serve, and to serve effectively in its limited way, up to our very day. Its originator,

Eugène Scribe, who flourished from 1815 to 1860, had the astuteness to gather together into one theatrical creation the many techniques which over several centuries had clearly contributed to the popular success of dramatic works.

Despite the romantic excesses of contemporaries like Hugo and Dumas the elder, who were pressing for new freedom in theatrical expression, Scribe based his own work upon a rational approach to his craft, and the belief that there were laws of dramatic structure which one could master. Like some nineteenth century Boileau, he stands at the threshold of modern theater, showing his juniors how to proceed. His legacy shaped all French plays, and many foreign ones, belonging to the mainstream of drama's popular development (as opposed to the experimental and elite), from the thesis plays and comedies of manners of Dumas the younger and Emile Augier, through the empty pleasantries of Victorien Sardou and the masterworks of Ibsen, right down to today's latest Parisian successes, as well as those of Broadway and Hollywood.

In Scribe's hands, the humble *vaudeville*, once a fairly unsophisticated mixture of sentimental and comic scenes with light lyrics sung to music of already existing popular songs, became one of the major forms of middle-class theater. Doing away with the songs, which found their way back and became glorified in the sentimental musical comedy (which is *our* major form of middle-class theater), he increased the importance of apparently well-motivated events, following swiftly upon one another, each reversing the effects of the preceding, so that the audience was kept constantly on edge. It was this form, the *vaudeville* (which is entirely unrelated to vaudeville as it was known in the United

States), that best served Feydeau, whether he called his play *vaudeville*, *comédie* or *comédie-vaudeville*.

Essential to the well-made play is its logical structure—indeed, the well-made play in Scribe's hands at least is almost nothing *but* structure, and action is its focal point: not action in a philosophical sense, but intrigue neither pure nor simple. Beginning at a point near its climax, the action rises and falls in a ceaseless movement following the fortunes and misfortunes of the hero and heroine, punctuated by reversals and surprises, and ending in a moving or thrilling "obligatory scene" (*scène à faire*) in which a secret, known to the audience, but withheld from certain characters, is finally revealed, and the true character of one or more personages is made clear.

This formula was brought to its peak of perfection by Victorien Sardou, a disciple of Scribe's, who learned his craft by reading the first act of a Scribe play, and then attempted to finish it by carrying the given elements to their logical dramatic conclusion. It is said that he worked backwards with his own plays, beginning with the dazzling "obligatory scene" and progressing crab-like to the exposition. Whatever his method, his career was brilliantly successful, and he was for many years a purveyor of plays to one of the greatest actresses of his era, Sarah Bernhardt.

Serious dramatists who believed in the mission of the theater branded him, as they did his master Scribe, a shallow entertainer. In a deathless expression, Shaw called his work "sardoodledom," stressing thereby the meaninglessness of the complicated structures of the well-made play. And yet most of the serious dramatists continued to draw on his techniques.

As the century came to an end, the French theater

was enjoying a healthy life. On the boulevards convention reigned supreme; fluffy *vaudevilles*, well-made plays, lilting operettas, and the last works of Dumas the younger and Augier seemed to suggest that the Second Empire spirit was not entirely dead. Aiding the authors to make the theater even more fascinating, if in an extradramatic way, were the great actors and actresses of the period. Following the lead (or perhaps leading the way) of everything else in *fin de siècle* France, they dramatized and posed their way through life, thrilling their publics horribly by tales of coffins used for beds, wild animals kept as pets, or the more banal stories of their fast-paced amorous adventures. Réjane, Bernhardt, Mounet-Sully are only the peaks, temperaments which made possible a rebirth of Romantic drama at the end of the century, with revivals of Hugo, the first production of Musset's masterly *Lorenzaccio* (with Sarah in the leading male role—for she specialized in male travesty, one might say, Hamlet being another of her major achievements), and the outstanding theatrical event of the 1890s which seemed to promise a rebirth of poetic theater, Edmond Rostand's *Cyrano* with the great Coquelin dominating the stage.

In the meantime, the Naturalists were making attempts to reform the theater. André Antoine's influential if short-lived Théâtre-Libre was founded in 1887, just one year after Feydeau's first popular success, *Tailleur pour dames*, in which one would be hard put to find any influence of the Naturalist aesthetic.

Likewise ostensibly absent from Feydeau's manner is that of the other reforming influence of its day, the poetic and Symbolist theater. The most notable of these was Lugné-Poë's Théâtre de l'Oeuvre which opened in 1893 with Maeterlinck's misty poetic *Pelléas et Méli-*

sande, and caused a scandal in 1896 (the year of *Le Dindon*) with Alfred Jarry's ferocious portrait of the bourgeois, *Ubu roi*.

The theater was bubbling with all kinds of activity. The Naturalists brought forth early fruit, and many of Antoine's dramatists became established writers for the bourgeois theater of the boulevards. Avant-gardists like Jarry, however, would have to wait another fifty years or more to come into their own in the theater. For the theater of the broad public was no more experimental in 1890 or 1900 than it is today. The Broadway, the Hollywood, of French theater was the middle-class theater of the boulevards, just as it is today. And then, as now, serious plays could be found on both boulevard and experimental stage—the very evening that Rostand's *Cyrano* triumphed at the Porte Saint Martin, his mistress Sarah Bernhardt was performing Octave Mirbeau's harsh naturalist play, Les Mauvais bergers, at her neighboring theater, the Renaissance.

Feydeau, disdaining the veristic prejudice of the Naturalists, and creating (as theater people have recognized today) a poetry very different from that of the Symbolists, derived his conventions from the bourgeois theater of the boulevards. Naturalism, he believed, ends up by banishing truth from the theater, and it overlooks the fact that all theater requires conventions. Using those developed by Scribe, Feydeau succeeded in creating theatrical truth and making, however covertly, a commentary on his contemporaries that, in company with *Ubu*, has outlived many of the more heavy-handed critiques of his more earnest colleagues. If we are to believe his admirers since the 1950s, Feydeau even succeeded in suggesting some bitter truths about the human condition as well. His own contemporaries, however, saw in him above all the entertainer and the brilliant theatrical craftsman.

The craft is apparent particularly in the construction of his full-length *vaudevilles* dealing with the vagaries and complexities of love in and out of wedlock. Of Feydeau's total *oeuvre*, two plays remained unfinished at his death—victims, no doubt, of his increasing laziness, but also of his demanding construction. Of the remaining 37 published works, fifteen are one-act pieces, some simple dialogues intended for salon performance, others sophisticated and witty pictures of the manners and morals of *fin de siècle* Paris. Most famous of the short plays, however, are the bitter portraits of marriage which the dramatist began to write toward the end of his active career: *Feu la mère de madame* (1908; Madam's Late Mother), *On purge bébé* (1910; *Going to Pot*), and *"Mais n'te promène donc pas toute nue!"* (1911; "Don't Walk Around Stark Naked!"). Many critics today would consider these deeply etched and black comedies of character to be Feydeau's masterpieces. Despite their bitter humor and absurd situations, they are less typical of the manner which earned Feydeau a reputation as the supreme geometrician of *vaudeville*.

The remaining 22 full-length plays, mostly in three acts, almost all embody at least certain aspects of this mathematical wizardry. The exceptions are two musical plays, *La Lycéenne* (1887; The Schoolgirl) and *L'Age d'or* (1905; The Golden Age), among the least successful of his works, one or two early plays, a comedy of character somewhat in the manner of Eugène Labiche (*Le Ruban*, 1894; The Decoration), and a drama, *Le Bourgeon* (1906; The Sprout). The full-length plays written after 1908 (*Le Circuit* [1909],

The Roadrace, and *Je ne trompe pas mon mari*, [1914], I'm Not Deceiving My Husband), both written with collaborators, are not among Feydeau's best works either. The remaining plays, however, are lively, fast-paced, tightly constructed mechanisms, the best of them whirling along at breakneck speed, yet never falling off the narrow track traced for them by their ingenious author. These plays, as well as the later comedies of character, are discussed in some detail in the last part of this volume. Since they all exhibit similar structural and thematic characteristics, I should like to deal with these in a synthesized way here and in the next chapter, in order to avoid needless and constant repetition in the section devoted to play summaries.

> To make a good *vaudeville*, [Feydeau explained] you take the most tragic situation possible, a situation fit to make a mortician shudder, and you try to bring out its burlesque side. There is no human drama which does not offer at least several comic aspects. That is why authors you call comic are always sad: they think "sad" first.[1]

The tragic side of great comedies has often been emphasized. One need only think of the behavior of any major character of Molière and its tragic consequences for others. Molière avoids tragedy by his much remarked *deus ex machina* endings, and of course by the general tone he adopts toward his maniacs. But given another tone, and without the help of artificial endings, *Tartuffe*, *L'Avare* and even *Le Bourgeois gentilhomme* could become at least middle-class drama if not full-blown tragedies.

Feydeau's "tragic" situations do not arise from character—at least they do not arise from specific charac-

ters within a given play. Rather they arise from the
nature of things, or from the character of the human
animal, given as he is to pleasure and particularly to animal pleasures. "Why don't you kill the animal in you?"
asks a married woman of her too insistent lover. "I
could never stand to hurt animals," he answers. Most
of Feydeau's men, and a few of the women, are very
kind to the animal in them, allowing it to lead them
where it will. And in order to give it a longer leash,
they lie time and again, and invent the most preposterous excuses for their guilty acts.

The fundamental situation in a Feydeau play is one
of deception. A husband is deceiving his wife, who discovers or suspects his infidelity and vows revenge
(*Monsieur chasse*, *Le Dindon*, *La Puce à l'oreille*, *Le
Système Ribadier*). A wife is deceiving her husband,
who discovers it and decides to divorce her (*La Main
passe*). A spouse is not discovered, or is finally forgiven,
in his (or her) deception (*L'Affaire Edouard*, *Champignol malgré lui*, *L'Hôtel du Libre-Echange*, *Tailleur
pour dames*, *La Dame de chez Maxim*, *La Duchesse
des Folies-Bergères*). A mistress is deceived or deceives
(*Un Fil à la patte*, *Occupe-toi d'Amélie*).

It is simple enough to imagine any of these situations
(which often recall the "secret" of the well-made
play) turning to tragedy or drama. One has only to
remember the serious plays dealing with adultery, illicit love and betrayal which have proliferated since
1850. If, instead of Lucette Gautier—the music-hall
singer to whom Bois-d'Enghien is tied by the leg (*Un
Fil à la patte*) with a cord stronger than matrimony,
and to whom he dares not admit his forthcoming marriage—we think of another Mlle Gautier, Marguerite,
the pathetic heroine of Dumas the younger's *La Dame*

aux camélias, we immediately realize the dramatic potential of such situations. Henry Arthur Jones, Arthur Wing Pinero, James A. Herne, Paul Hervieu, Maurice Donnay, Hermann Sudermann are only a few of Feydeau's contemporaries to treat similar themes in a serious key, and with Paul Claudel's *Partage de midi*, adultery approaches sublimity.

With Feydeau we are at the antipodes of sublimity, but occasionally, as in *Le Dindon* or *Le Bourgeon*, he takes time to consider the characters seriously, and the tone is close to that of drama.

Deception is not always voluntary. A staple of the *vaudeville* had for many years been the *quiproquo* literally the taking of this for that. Two characters meet, each believing the other is someone else, or that he is pursuing a subject different from the one he is actually pursuing. Some of Feydeau's most hilarious scenes are based upon such situations. His earliest plays, in fact, often take such a misunderstanding as the foundation of their action. In *Les Fiancés de Loches* (1888; The Fiancés from Loches) three provincials come to a Paris employment agency for servants, thinking they are in a marriage bureau, because the defunct matrimonial service on the floor above has left a note directing its clients to the floor below. The employment agency hires them out to a doctor, his fiancée, and an old maid sister whom they believe to be their future spouses. The familiarity of the "servants" and their astonishment at the things they are asked to do by their fiancés account for much of the humor in the play. Feydeau's first play in collaboration with Maurice Desvallières, who was to co-sign several of his most famous works, *Les Fiancés de Loches* runs lickety-split from beginning to end, each scene more absurdly insane than the last. Without the almost violent incongruity and speed, which liken it to a Marx Brothers' film, the constant reverting to the same technique would wear thin.

The simpler *Chat en poche* (1888; A Bird in Hand) derives its comic effects from a misunderstanding on the part of Monsieur Pacarel, a wealthy bourgeois who had telegraphed a friend in Bordeaux to send him the tenor Dujeton, who has made such a hit in the provincial city. Pacarel hopes to become the singer's protector and then "sell" him to the Paris Opera on condition that they perform his own daughter's new version of *Faust*. A young man arrives, actually the son of the friend in Bordeaux, who never received the telegram. The son is surprised that Pacarel wishes to offer him a huge allowance, and humors the wealthy man when he asks him to sing. Everyone is astounded at his lack of voice, but his true identity is only discovered at the end. The young man is also confused as to the identity of the woman he is pursuing, for he recognizes Pacarel's wife as a woman he had met on a bus the day before, and attempts to court her. But since he was introduced to the two-family ménage at once, he thinks she is Amandine—the wife of Pacarel's friend—rather than Pacarel's wife, Marthe.

Madness, absurdity and *quiproquos* galore keep the play light and generally fast-moving. Occasionally, however, it becomes repetitious and dull in the forced humor of the situations. Feydeau had not yet found the precise formula which was to make his name only four or five years later.

That formula includes a plot which is complicated by a number of subplots, shaken by surprises and *coups de théâtre*, suddenly reversed or at least threatened by unexpected (but well-prepared and therefore at least subconsciously expected) incidents and finally, after a mad romp usually taking place in the second act where the chaos reaches its summit, slowly, meticulously, clearly and cleverly untied in a lengthy denouement.

Discussing, in an interview, his recipe for a *vaudeville*, Feydeau compares himself to a pharmacist preparing a prescription: "I put into my pill a gram of imbroglio, a gram of libertinage, a gram of observation."[2]

Observation supplies themes and characters and gives them life, libertinage whets the appetites of the blasé theatergoer and lightens the tone, but it is the imbroglio or action which either melds the elements into a successful theater piece or condemns them to the bookshelf or the drawer. "Theater is above all the development of an action," Feydeau wrote in a letter to a friend, "and action is the very basis of *vaudeville* and melodrama."[3] Those two much-maligned forms of theater, if not so sublime as tragedy or so socially useful as comedy (although both claims might be contested) are at least equally close to the ground base of theater. Indeed, this may account for their "vulgarity," for they are theater rather than drama. Feydeau, a number of times, inveighed against theater as pulpit, and dialogue as literature. Both tendencies, he claimed, killed theater.

Today, when much theater has turned its back upon the literary and the explicitly ideological, Feydeau seems quite modern, despite his *belle époque* décor and costumes. He discovered, at a time when serious theater was thrashing out social problems and art theater was lost in poetic fantasy, that movement was the "essential condition of theater." By this he meant the

actual physical movement of the actors on the stage, as
well as the more "Aristotelian" development of action
from beginning to middle to end.

> I am in possession of a play as a chess player is
> in possession of his chessboard [he claimed]. The
> successive positions my pawns (that is to say, my
> characters) have occupied onstage are constantly
> present in my mind.[4]

Both action and movement are of prime importance
in a Feydeau play, and the author was constantly in
command of both. Indeed, like the great dramatists of
the past, Feydeau was the director of his own plays,
and he insisted that the actors perform the play he had
imagined and not some other. For this reason, the most
intricate movements, stage tricks, or intonations are
noted minutely. In *Occupe-toi d'Amélie* one section of
speech is even given in musical notation, so that the
actor will use the proper intonation. The texts of some
of the plays run many pages longer than most scripts,
because the movement is spelled out in great detail. To
fail to follow the author's instructions is to court trouble, for suddenly an actor or an object may turn up in
the wrong place. The physical movement, like the
development of the action, is constructed with a mathematical precision which cannot be upset with impunity.

So wedded was Feydeau to this concept that he refused to allow cuts in his plays. On one occasion when
the director finally summoned the courage to send
someone to ask him to cut a bit from a play, Feydeau
inquired coldly, "How many minutes must be cut?"
"About ten." "And how many pages does that rep-

resent?" "Twenty pages," was the reply. "Very well," responded the dramatist. "Tell them to begin on page 21."

Following the model of the well-made play, Feydeau always begins his action near its climax. In the first act, which is almost entirely devoted to exposition, each scene is usually created with three ends in mind: to make clear the fundamental situation at the play's outset, i.e., the deception or misunderstanding and what led up to it; to prepare the complex situations which will arise in the following acts in such a way that they will seem logical, inevitable, yet surprising; and to amuse the audience with situations which are droll or preposterous, but which always have a ring of truth. In his greatest works, while doing all this, Feydeau also succeeds in giving us insights into character, and flashes of a nightmarish picture of the human predicament in which men are victims of a wildly irrational universe.

Toward the end of Act I, the main action begins, usually set in motion by some fault, mistake, misjudgment, or lie. In Act II the results of this mistake are witnessed, usually in a bachelor apartment or a hotel, occasionally in a salon or bedroom. But wherever the scene, it has the intimacy of a subway station at rush hour, as the major characters from Act I appear, disappear, and reappear with a rigorous logic, often coming and going at breakneck speed through the three, four, five or six doors which the author usually provides. In several cases new, and incidental, comic characters are brought into this act, but their presence is always felt as likely or even necessary.

It is in Act II, if not before, that Feydeau brings into play most rigorously the rule he established for himself:

> When writing a play, I seek among my characters
> the ones who should not run into each other. And
> they are precisely the ones I bring into a confron-
> tation as soon as possible . . .[5]

Such a rule is fundamental to all drama, and particularly to melodrama and the Romantic drama which is
so close to it. Without the accidental or coincidental
meetings—so much better avoided—the majority of
Romantic dramas would not get far along, or at least
would not come to a head. Feydeau, as so often, has
taken a standard theatrical device and pushed it to the
limits of verisimilitude—or beyond.

In the similar instances, of characters who have just
been pronounced either at death's door, irretrievably
ill, or in some impossibly distant place, and who are
promptly announced, Feydeau is again indebted to a
device of the *drame*. But in the Romantic play, instead
of bringing about amusing complications, such an
encounter may draw down upon the characters the
most dire results, at which we are scarcely disposed to
laugh—unless, of course, we see the artifice through a
late twentieth-century eye rather than the pathos
through an eye of the 1830s. In Hugo's finest poetic
drama, *Ruy Blas* (1838) the poor lackey in love with
the queen has decided to die, and laments, "I shall never
see her again. Never!" She immediately enters by a hidden door—right into the trap prepared for her. One
could scarcely imagine a situation more Feydeau-like in
its outlines, but the tone is far from light.

Even classical tragedy, with its action bearing on the
inner man and his perception of truth, is not immune
from this rule. One wonders what would have happened had Oedipus not met the sphinx, or not happened

to have learned the answer to the riddle, or even having accomplished all that, if he had not gone on to Thebes and met Jocasta. Cocteau, in his beautiful modern treatment of the tale, *La Machine infernale*, plays upon the irony of such chance meetings. But Oedipus does not fear these encounters as do the characters of comedy. Indeed, tragic characters are often unaware of the implications of the meetings even while they are taking place, for the tragic meeting is one whose true meaning is revealed at the end, and only in retrospect does the hero know that he might well have feared it. The comic meeting is anticipated with distaste or experienced with displeasure.

The worst meeting of all is that between the guilty husband and his suspicious wife, or the suspecting husband and his wife caught in compromising circumstances. Such a scene corresponds to the "obligatory scene" of the well-made play, in which the secret explodes and we, the spectators, witness the encounter which seemed inevitable from the beginning. Scribe customarily placed such a scene near the end of his play and followed it with a lightning-like denouement, and often one which contained a new surprise. Feydeau most often places this high point of discovery at the end of the second act, leaving all of act three for a lengthy, quick-paced and very complicated untying of the knots.

No playwright of integrity lives totally by a formula, and all of Feydeau's plays cannot be pressed within the confines of such a mold. In *La Dame de chez Maxim*, for example, the revelation scene does not take place until the Scribean moment just before the final curtain. In some plays, indeed in almost all of them, there is not one secret, there are a number, and they are set off like time bombs all along the course of the play, exploding one after the other.

In *Occupe-toi d'Amélie* the major secret is that of Marcel's trumped-up marriage to Amélie, so that he may receive the inheritance held for him by his Uncle Van Putzeboum. The Dutch uncle only discovers the truth at the final curtain, but, ironically, Marcel has really been married to Amélie by this time, thanks to the machinations of Amélie's former lover, Etienne, whose pretended false wedding ceremony is a second secret. And this secret arises from his discovery of yet another secret: that Amélie, whom he had left in the care of his best friend, Marcel, has been to bed with the man. Whether anything had transpired in bed is yet another secret, but one which is destined never to be revealed, since both parties were quite drunk.

Among the most typical full-length plays, we may consider there to be two types. *La Puce à l'oreille*, *Un Fil à la patte*, *La Dame de chez Maxim*, *Occupe-toi d'Amélie*, and *Champignol malgré lui* have large casts, extremely complex action, and incidents which can only be described as extravagant. In some of them there are even crowd scenes: the second act of *Champignol* includes military drill, and that of *La Dame de chez Maxim* takes place at a provincial party with a wealth of provincial types, while the first scene of Act III in *Occupe-toi d'Amelie* shows a wedding taking place in the city hall.

The other group of plays, invariably treating domestic problems (whereas three of the first group show the world of the *cocotte*), has smaller casts, a slightly simpler (and sometimes much simpler) plot, and is sometimes more realistic in tone, even approaching at times comedy of character with a foretaste of the bitter portraits that are featured in the last short plays. The plays of this group always begin in middle-class households where all is not well between husband and wife, although this is not always immediately apparent to both spouses. The action starts somewhat more slowly than in the plays of the first group, giving more time for the creation of character. Gradually it builds to a crisis situation which usually reaches a peak near the end of Act I. These are the plays in which the wronged wife (with the sole exception of the vixen in *L'Hôtel du Libre-Echange*) cries out that she will avenge herself and put a pair of horns on her husband's head. Usually there is a lover-in-waiting (normally the husband's best friend) ready to leap at the opportunity.

By contrast, the one wronged wife of the more "extravagant" plays, Lucienne (in *La Puce à l'oreille*), once she feels quite convinced (although erroneously) that her husband is deceiving her, no longer has the inclination to throw herself at her would-be lover.

Beginning in a crisis situation, the extravagant plays move at a quick tempo from one complication to another, aggravated by inopportune arrivals, unexpected revelations, cowardly lies, or wrong decisions. At the beginning of *La Dame de chez Maxim*, Dr. Petypon wakes up to find himself under a sofa and a *cocotte*, La Môme Crevette, in his bed. His wife pops in and out, Crevette finally gets rid of the superstitious woman by pretending to be an angel sent to give her a message from heaven. Petypon's uncle, a general, arrives and mistakes Crevette for his nephew's wife. A former lover of Crevette comes to set up details of a duel with Petypon, who apparently had an encounter with him the night before, although the doctor was too drunk to remember it. The general-uncle invites Crevette to take charge of an engagement party he is giving in his country chateau for another niece, and, as the curtain falls Petypon sets off for the chateau, hoping to prevent Crevette from making a slip. At the same time, Mme Petypon receives an invitation the general had written earlier, and she too sets off for the chateau.

In each play of this "extravagant" group, the *quiproquo* plays an important part, and brings about, in Act II a meeting of almost all the characters from the first act.

After a sometimes bitter picture of married life, the more realistic plays gain momentum and finally bring all characters together again in Act II. As in the first act, however, the complications of Act II are here simplified by the smaller number of characters available and by the slightly less extravagant tone which prevails. It is in the second act that both plays most clearly use the seesaw movement which is typical of the well-made play. The fortunes of the man or woman who is threatened with discovery rise and fall with a relentless rhythm, as doors open and close, characters from Act I spilling over from one room to another in the hotel or bachelor apartment where Act II most often takes place. From one unlikely coincidence to the next, the action rises to the climactic unmasking scene, without, however, striking us as unlikely, for each moment is so well prepared, so logically brought about, that it is only when confronted by the absurd action itself that we are aware of its absurdity. The unmasking is emotionally satisfying to us because we have been led to expect it, however dimly, and we experience it as inevitable.

In Act II of either group of plays, the most dazzling spatial geometry is developed. With great care, the author describes each move of each character, never misplacing one of them. Perhaps the most spectacular exhibition of this uncanny skill is found in *La Dame de chez Maxim*. As the curtain rises on the grand salon of the general's chateau in Touraine, there are no less than fourteen named characters onstage, along with an unspecified number of military officers, guests, valets, and a chorus of children. In all, about thirty actors are present. Skipping from group to group, Feydeau gives us lengthy realistic bits of conversation which seem quite logically to be the focal point of the room as we listen. As was his custom, he numbers the positions of the actors as they appear from left to right of the stage (as seen from the audience, *not*, as is the custom in the United States, from the actor's right and left). As a footnote to one scene, for example, he indicates:

> La Môme Crevette, in the center of the group, in front of the buffet. Around her, a bit upstage, Mesdames Hautignol (1), Ponant (2), Virette (3), next to the buffet. The baroness is at the right end of the buffet, and across from her is Emile, and a valet serving refreshments. Clémentine is a bit to the side, between Mme Hautignol and Mme Ponant. Petypon is between the easy chair, in which the Duchess is seated, and the buffet.
>
> (II, 1)

This is only an indication of one small group in the scene. The rest of the thirty actors have been as carefully placed, as will be the other five or six yet to enter. With unerring instinct, the author brings one character across the stage, another up to the buffet and a third from one chair to another, and two minutes later effects an equally intricate move with four or five other actors, keeping the stage constantly alive and true to life, and never forgetting where he has left a character.

This mastery of the physical movement corresponds, on the visual level, to the mastery of mounting action which Feydeau reveals at every moment of his play, but most particularly in the hectic second acts.

A radical change from the Scribean formula is the lengthy unravelling of the action—necessary, at least in part, because the action has become so complicated. Occasionally the third act, most of which is devoted to the denouement, seems to slow down, particularly after the frenetic action of Act II. In some plays, however, like *La Dame de chez Maxim* or *Occupe-toi d'Amélie*, where the "obligatory scene" is postponed to the third act, the action continues to mount. In the latter play, the action of Act III is totally different from that of the preceding acts. In the first two acts, we see Marcel's efforts to deceive his uncle from Holland, and his apparent deception of his friend, Etienne, who had entrusted Amélie to his care. From the end of Act II, where a revelation takes place which brings to a resolution the action of the first part of the play (Etienne discovers Amélie's supposed infidelity with Marcel), the play changes course. No longer fearful of the uncle's discovery, we follow Etienne's plan for revenge, as he really marries Amélie to Marcel in a ceremony he had claimed was only make-believe. *Occupe-toi d'Amélie* is almost two different plays, the first in two acts, the second in two scenes. The second scene of each is a bedroom, perhaps an indication that Feydeau realized the double structure he was building, for this is his only play with two bedroom scenes.

This is an extreme example, no doubt, but it is indicative of a tendency in all Feydeau's works. The first two acts are involved with the major action which rises to the climax and usual unmasking at the end of Act II. Act III, which unties the snaggled knot, is also concerned with a number of related questions, and somehow deflects the action from its major course. In *La Puce à l'oreille*, for example, the first two acts show Lucienne's efforts to trap her husband whom she incorrectly believes is deceiving her. By the end of Act II it is she who is begging his forgiveness for having been found in the hotel with another man. She still does not understand how his suspenders could have been left at the Hôtel du Minet Galant, and that mystery is finally cleared up in Act III. But most of the final act is devoted to resolving the perplexities of the double identity of Chandebise-Poche (Lucienne's husband is the spit and image of the hotel bellboy), an action related to the first one, but different, after all.

In *Un Fil à la patte*, the major action concerns Bois-d'Enghien's efforts to keep apart his lives as lover of the singer Lucette Gautier, and as husband-to-be of the Baroness Duverger's daughter. His task is rendered difficult when the Baroness invites Lucette to sing at the engagement party. By the end of Act II, both worlds have fallen about Bois-d'Enghien's ears, and our curiosity on that score has been satisfied. The third act shows the young man extricating himself from his liaison with Lucette, avoiding the threats of a jealous Latin American general, and patching up things with his fiancée. These are all threads which require tying, but they are not the main string we were following in the first two acts.

As we might expect in a theater which depends upon plot and movement, Feydeau's comedy is largely one of situation. He uses comedy of character and language as well. The former is found chiefly in the later short plays. The latter is a minor form in his plays, except as it relates to situation or character.

Indeed, Feydeau, unlike more facile writers of comedy or farce, refused to use comic material simply to make his audience laugh. He required that it arise naturally from the situations or characters. René Peter, who co-authored with Feydeau the last full-length play he signed, *Je ne trompe pas mon mari* (1914), recounts his first reading of the manuscript to the master. Peter, hoping Feydeau could help him place the play, had brought it for him to see, and was overjoyed when the famous dramatist consented to rework the play and sign it with the young man. Peter himself recounts his reading of the play:

> I'll never forget how, in the middle of my reading, he suddenly interrupted me:
> "Ah! charming! That is truly charming . . . What a beautiful line—witty, original."
> Naturally I was in seventh heaven. He concluded:
> "You'll have to cut it."
> I was dazed.
> "Cut it? But why?"
> "Because it doesn't arise from the situation. It's theater wit . . . And that, never. It's a witticism. A thing to be avoided above all else."
> "Then, one should never be witty?"
> "Yes, when it comes about naturally, when the play demands it. Otherwise, it interrupts the movement."[6]

Comic language in Feydeau reflects an imperfect command of standard French, as in the case of the

numerous foreign or provincial characters who massa-
cre the language. Or else it arises from a distraction or
an emotional tension of the characters, as in the case of
Mathieu in *L'Hôtel du Libre-Echange*. Unable to speak
without stuttering when it is raining, Mathieu gra-
ciously explains his unexpected visit to the Pinglets:

> PINGLET: A peine arrivé, votre première visite est
> pour nous!
> MATHIEU: Dame! vous pensez bien, mon cher,
> qu'aucu . . . hum, mon cher qu'aucu . . . hum!
> PINGLET: Qu'est-ce qu'il dit?
> MATHIEU: Qu'aucune visite ne me tenait plus à
> coeur.
>
> (I, XIII)

> PINGLET: Scarcely have you arrived and your first
> call is on us!
> MATHIEU: Of course! You can understand, my
> dear that no . . . hum! my dear, that no . . .
> hum!
> PINGLET: What's he saying?
> MATHIEU: That no visit was closer to my heart.

As Bergson observes, true comic language cannot be
translated: in this scene, "that no," in French
"qu'aucu . . ." sounds like Mathieu is calling Pinglet,
"my dear cuckold."

But plays on words are usually reserved for the
uneducated classes in these plays, the servants and maids
who do not quite understand what their masters are
referring to and interpret them freely. A valet in an
early play, for example, hearing that his mistress is
playing some Beethoven, deforms it to the nearest
recognizable expression he can extract from the already

deformed French pronunciation of a German name: *bête à veine* (lucky beast).

In his masterly study of *Laughter*, the French philosopher Bergson, who was Feydeau's contemporary, considers the situational comedy of *vaudeville* to be made up of three principal techniques: repetition, inversion and interference of series. These are, indeed, the methods which Feydeau learned from his predecessors in the *vaudeville* form, and which are used most frequently by him.

Repetition of words is a much used comic device in classical comedy. With *vaudeville*, it is rather the repetition of situations which strikes us. When a situation is repeated sufficiently, it becomes not only comic, but begins to put on the appearance of a universal plot, particularly if viewed through the eyes of the character at the center of the situation. Bois-d'Enghien might well feel himself the victim of a plot to reveal to his mistress the secret of his engagement, for almost every time he turns around a new character has entered and produced a copy of the morning *Figaro*, which contains both a review of Lucette's latest concert, and news of Bois-d'Enghien's forthcoming marriage. One after another, he seizes the newspaper from the hands of the surprised bearer and stuffs it into his own coat.

A more dire use of repetition occurs in *Champignol malgré lui*, when the true Champignol reports for military duty, not knowing that St.-Florimond has already reported in his name (having been found in Mme Champignol's bedroom and therefore mistaken for her husband). The sergeant orders the barber to cut Champignol's hair, but the sergeant is referring to St.-Florimond whom he believes to be Champignol, while the barber only knows the true Champignol. Each time the sergeant encounters St.-Florimond, he orders a shorter haircut, which the barber executes upon the true Champignol, until the latter is totally bald. At this point the sergeant comes upon Champignol and orders him punished for cutting his hair so short.

These are examples of relatively minor incidents which are repeated. Important situations are repeated within a play also. In *Un Fil à la patte*, and again in *La Puce à l'oreille*, the jealous Latin American runs in and out pursuing suspected rivals. In almost every play, a kind of repetition takes place in Act II where everyone from the first act turns up in the same place, and often with similar motives. The classic technique of repeating the actions of the masters on the level of the servants is also used, but we are in more democratic times: the plan of the master to deceive his wife with some other woman in a seedy hotel is paralleled by a similar project between a servant girl and the master's nephew (Camille and Antoinette in *La Puce à l'oreille*; Maxime and Victoire in *L'Hôtel du Libre-Echange*).

Feydeau's use of inversion is more frequent. It underlies the humor of a play like *Dormez, je le veux!* (Sleep, I command it!), in which a servant hypnotizes his master and makes him perform all the household duties while he himself eats and relaxes. Somewhat more sophisticated are the lovers who are jealous of husbands (Massenay in *La Main passe*), servants who are mistaken for masters (Poche in *La Puce à l'oreille*; the valet in *Tailleur pour dames*), or *cocottes* who are mistaken for wives (Crevette in *La Dame de chez Maxim*, who plays hostess at the general's chateau, while Petypon's real wife, who had been invited to be hostess, is thought to be offensive and even crazy by the guests who consider her an interloper). Another kind of inversion is seen in characters like De Fontanet in *Un Fil à la patte*. Afflicted with bad breath, only De Fontanet is unaware of it, and becomes particularly comical when he complains of the bad breath of others, or when he suggests reviving the fainting Lucette by breathing in her face.

Feydeau also exploits the theme of the deceiver deceived, another variation of the inversion formula. In *Le Système Ribadier*, the husband mesmerizes his wife so that he may go off to visit his mistress. When the wife leads him to believe that she has been violated while asleep on countless occasions, he is placed in the cuckold's role he had imposed on his mistress's husband. In *Occupe-toi d'Amélie*, Marcel, although unwittingly, has spent the night in bed with Amélie, who had been entrusted to him by Etienne. In the end he finds himself unwillingly married to the *cocotte*. Bois-d'Enghien (*Un Fil à la patte*) spends much of Acts I and II attempting to keep the truth from his mistress Lucette, and deluding his fiancée Viviane into believing that he is a model of virtue. When Lucette tricks him into a compromising position, grabs him in her arms crying out, "Ah! No one has ever made love to me like that!" and allows all the guests at the engagement party to enter the room, we are amused and quite satisfied that the young man has gotten what he deserved. The same is true of Pontagnac in *Le Dindon*. The title itself (a *dindon*, or turkey, is the one left empty-handed at the end) indicates the role that Pontagnac will ultimately play after having attempted to force his attentions upon his friend's wife.

The technique which Bergson calls an interference

of a series results in the most famous of all *vaudeville* devices: the *quiproquo*. Bergson describes this as the coincidence, at some point, of two independent series. For example, a near-sighted journalist comes to interview Mme Paginet who has recently been awarded the legion of honor. At the same time, Dr. Paginet believes erroneously that *he* has received the award, and comes out to meet the journalist. The resulting misunderstanding, which takes place at the intersecting point of the two independent series, is a *quiproquo*, and an extremely amusing one. The journalist finds Mme Paginet to be charming, but somewhat masculine, and is astounded that she should choose to dress as a man. Paginet, in turn, is surprised at the observations of the interviewer:

> RASANVILLE: Have you any children?
> PAGINET: Alas, no.
> RASANVILLE: Then I can't put down that you have known the joys of childbirth.
> PAGINET: Ah, that would be difficult.
>
> (II, VIII)

Examples of *quiproquo* abound. In some plays it is the fundamental situation. The charming one act play, *Amour et piano*, brings together a young man hoping to establish a liaison with a music-hall singer, and a young lady expecting her new piano teacher. More extended developments of the same kind of situation occur in *Les Fiancés de Loches*, *Chat en poche*, and *Champignol malgré lui*, where for most of the play the mistaken identity persists, and is even compounded in the last mentioned play with variations of the device, permitted by the presence of the true Champignol.

Even when the *quiproquo* does not underlie the entire play, this legacy from the well-made play turns up frequently to complicate the lives of the protagonists. Time and again Lucienne and Tournel, at the Hôtel du Minet Galant (*La Puce à l'oreille*), believe they are talking with Lucienne's husband, Chandebise, when in truth they are dealing with the simple-minded hotel bellboy, Poche. Conversely, the hotel owner mistreats Chandebise as though he were Poche. The marriage scene of *Occupe-toi d'Amélie* brings together the mayor who is ready to perform a true wedding ceremony, and Amélie, Marcel and their friends who believe the mayor is only play-acting.

In *Le Dindon* three series coincide, producing a particularly amusing moment: (1) the clients of the hotel are trying to sleep but are disturbed by the ringing of a bell from one of the rooms; (2) Dr. Pinchard and his deaf wife are trying to sleep, but a bell is ringing somewhere in their room; (3) Lucienne and Pontagnac are waiting in the adjacent room hoping to trap the the former's husband, after having planted bells under the mattress to signal the moment when husband and mistress would presumably be in bed. Each of the three groups is mistaken in its assumptions about the other. A fourth group (the guilty husband and his would-be mistress) is represented by the mistress, Maggy, who, having been mistakenly given the same room as the Pinchards, is, during the above melée, hiding in the bathroom.

Situational comedy, such as that found in farce and *vaudeville*—the comedy at which Feydeau excelled—has not traditionally stood high in critical esteem. It is placed above the lowly pun, but well below the level of comedy of character. The reason for this is given by Bergson. The *purpose* of laughter (and hence of comedy), he declares, is to correct behavior that is dehumanized or antisocial. At the base of all comedy, in the Bergsonian view, lies some distraction which renders a character momentarily (or temperamentally) incapable of reacting in a living human way. He fails to adapt to changing circumstances, and like a robot or a machine, continues what he has always done, when he should have been adaptable. In simplest terms, he falls into a hole or slips on a banana peel. On a more sophisticated level, he betrays his mania (which has dehumanized him, made him a miser, a misanthrope, a dreamer, etc.) in more complex acts and words. In comedy of character, comic acts and words derive always from character.

Situation comedy, on the other hand, reveals a distraction in *things*, life is seen as a mechanism with interchangeable pieces and reversible effects. The mathematical piling up of objects or events, with their repetitions, inversions and interferences, underlines the mechanical aspect of life itself which is unaware and comic. Unlike the comic of character, says Bergson, situational comedy corrects nothing. It was simply invented to make us laugh, because we enjoy laughter. It is therefore somewhat divorced from life and reality and does not, like character comedy, plunge its roots deep in life:

> Thus we can understand *vaudeville* which is to real life what the puppet is to a man who can walk, a very artificial exaggeration of a certain natural stiffness of things. The string connecting

it to real life is slender indeed. It is scarcely more than a game, subordinated like all games to a convention which must be first accepted.[7]

In the *belle époque*, Bergson's observations may have been acceptable, but in the last half of the twentieth century life *has* become so dehumanized that Feydeau's plays stand today almost as a revelation of the threatening universe in which we live. Viewing a revival of *La Main passe*, Jean Cocteau exclaimed, "It's a real nightmare . . . pure Kafka."[8]

Everything allows us to concur, for life seen through two World Wars, and through the perspectives established by the theater of the absurd, particularly that of Ionesco, suggests that there is indeed a natural stiffness of things, life itself *is* given to distractions, and man is all too often the victim of these bad jokes. Instead of relegating situation comedy to an inferior position, writers like Beckett and Ionesco have suggested that it has metaphysical implications. It is these that we now can see in Feydeau, and that his contemporaries were not sensitive to.

Not every *vaudeville* suggests a truth beyond itself. Not every clown is representative of man lost in a meaningless universe. It takes the genius of a Chaplin or a Beckett to create such a clown. In the *vaudeville* it takes a craftsman who is master enough of the form to send it reeling into the void at breakneck speed. But it takes more than that, for theatrical abstraction, no matter how perfect, could not speak meaningfully to us. Despite his scorn for the Naturalists, despite his brilliant form in which the loose strings of life are at last neatly tied up, and everything is arranged artistically, we cannot overlook Feydeau, the realist. For Feydeau's

characters, the situations in which they find themselves, and the words they speak, derive from a keen,
sometimes kindly, sometimes caustic, observation of
life. It is this which gives its strength and dimension to
his brilliant mechanisms.

THE TASTE FOR TRUTH

In March, 1887, André Antoine began the rare and scattered performances of his Théâtre-Libre which were to revolutionize contemporary theater practice and exercise an influence over dramatic writing to our very day. Eclectic in repertoire and style, Antoine nonetheless leaned toward plays of the Realistic and Naturalistic mode. The Théâtre-Libre became synonymous with the effort to make the theater a faithful imitation of life as it is lived—often at the lowest levels. Shocking their audiences with real sides of meat dripping blood, or plays depicting double adultery verging on incest, the supporters of the "slice of life" theater looked down on the conventions which had developed during the course of the nineteenth century and were by now ossified in the productions of writers like Sardou and the aging Dumas the younger. Almost beneath their scorn were the frivolous farces and *vaudevilles* which were amusing their thoughtless contemporaries on the boulevards.

In the December preceding the founding of the Théâtre-Libre, Feydeau's first major success was produced,
Tailleur pour dames.[1] The young author would no
doubt have been the first to express surprise if anyone
had suggested even the remotest relationship between
his light comedies and the heavy-handed dramas in
Antoine's early repertoire. Indeed, he later quite
frankly declared his disagreement with the Naturalist
aesthetic which denied the importance of convention.

Despite the difference in form and tone, Feydeau's
comedies owe as much as do the most Naturalistic
works of his day to a rare gift of observation. Trans-
posing reality, as all art does, pushing it to a paroxysm
of madness, treating serious themes obliquely, Feydeau
created works which, ironically enough, have survived
much longer than the serious and pretentious works of
his denigrators. Exercising our humor, our imagination, and even our intelligence, trivial farces of the
turn of the century turn out to be a revealing commentary on ourselves, going far beyond the limited visions
of pure Realism and Naturalism.

"He loved only truth and the natural," declared Feydeau's last collaborator, René Peter.[2] It takes little per-
spicacity to see the truth beneath the bright surface.
Feydeau's theater reflects a world he knew intimately—
that of the high-living bourgeois of *belle époque* Paris,
spiced with incursions into the world of the demimonde, and visits from foreigners and provincials.

The moment we enter the living rooms and bedrooms
of these idle rich, we are overwhelmed with signs of
opulence: French doors, large bay windows, stylish
furnishings filling all available space, abundant bric-a-
brac, clocks, paintings, telephones, electric bells, and
often tables laden with the food so extravagantly con-

sumed during the *belle époque*. In lengthy stage directions, the author details the precise stylings, colors and
positions of most furnishings, outdoing in thorough-
ness the most painstaking realists.

Into these settings Feydeau brings settled or unsettled couples, family groups bristling with uncles and
in-laws, surrounded by lovers, friends, visitors, servants, intruders, and hangers-on. In equally middle-
class luxury we find the gay world of the *cocottes*,
with *their* lovers, servants, relatives and parasites. Into
whatever world we are plunged, we note the marks of
veracity in setting, costume, manner and language. Like
Molière, Feydeau makes each character speak the language—or gibberish—which is appropriate to his station or profession.

Particularly colorful in their language are the *cocottes*—fresh, vivacious young women devoted to entertainment (most of them are singers or dancers) and to
making themselves as appetizing as possible to their
potential protectors. Often inventive, always spirited,
the Crevettes, Lucettes, and Amélies of this world express themselves freely, with a linguistic frankness and
down-to-earthness which endears them to us midst the
affectations of some of the bourgeois women. Materialistic when on business, they are devoted in love, and
capable of great ingenuity in order to advance their
lot in life. When called upon to do so, they can impersonate (with only slight comic lapses) the ladies of high
society. Crevette must do so when she plays the part of
Petypon's wife at her "uncle's" chateau. Amélie is
astonishingly "classy" when she first makes the
acquaintance of the wealthy uncle who holds the purse
strings to her friend Marcel's inheritance. She adopts
a Comédie-Française accent, a poetic vocabulary, and

a modest manner which cause Van Putzeboum to exclaim, "Ah! Chaste girl! She's pure as gold!"

A second later Amélie catches herself answering Putzeboum's query, "Do you like jewelry?" with a familiar "You bet!" But she is able to twist the words into another meaning and continue the comedy.

Some critics have claimed that Feydeau's characters have no trade or profession. Jean-Louis Barrault, whose much-praised revival of *Occupe-toi d'Amélie* in 1948 signaled the rise of Feydeau to almost classic status, claims that there are few professions represented aside from those of *cocottes*, policemen and maids. These are workers who establish order, he observes: "glandular order, domestic order, public order."[3] Yet almost every character in this brimming world is identified at some moment by his work. We are unaware, perhaps, of our hero's profession because he rarely thinks of it himself. His life is consecrated not to work, but to pleasure. There are, indeed, fortunate young playboys who live on a private income and never raise a finger. But they are few, and most of the bourgeois we meet must at some time or other at least cast a thought upon their workaday world.

Moulineaux, the "hero" of *Tailleur pour dames*, is a doctor. True, he spends a good deal of his time pretending to be a tailor in order to hide the truth from his mistress's husband. But he spends time in his office too—for it is there that he finds it easiest to meet with his mistress, who has a weekly appointment to see her doctor. The most notable doctor is Petypon in *La Dame de chez Maxim*, a serious, solid, professional who, making the mistake of accompanying a friend one night to Maxim's, gets drunk and wakes up the next morning to find the irrepressible Môme Crevette in his bed, and a duel on his hands—none of the reasons for which can he remember from the night before. The "ecstatic chair," newest electrical gadget for the cure and pleasure of his patients, which he has no doubt purchased at great expense, attests to his professional seriousness.

Other doctors weave through the plays, occupying now a major role (Saint-Galmier in *Les Fiancés de Loches*, Paginet in *Le Ruban*), now a subsidiary one (Finache in *La Puce à l'oreille*, Pinchard in *Le Dindon*). But whether major or minor, the doctors give medical or moral advice, look to the operation of their hospital, or discuss their medical theories. The battered husband of Feydeau's last play, *Hortense a dit: "Je m'en fous!"* is not only said to be a dentist, he is actually shown practicing his profession. Torturing his patients with the drill, filling their mouths with implements and instruments, Dr. Follbraguet is finally so exasperated by his impossible wife that he walks out, abandoning his last terrified patient, who remains onstage, gurgling and gasping through his propped-open mouth.

Chandebise, in *La Puce à l'oreille*, is an insurance agent, and some of the complications in his life arise from his professional interest in insuring the jealous and passionate Latin American, Homenides. Paillardin (*L'Hôtel du Libre-Echange*), an architect, also finds his life complicated by his professional commitments: he must spend the night in a hotel room supposedly haunted by ghosts—the same hotel to which his best friend intends to bring Mme Paillardin.

The initial complication of *Le Dindon* also arises because of business relations: When Pontagnac has the audacity to follow a beautiful woman into her very apartment in order to woo her, he discovers to his surprise that her husband is an old friend. This allows him to pretend he has come on a visit, and the naive husband believes him.

In *"Mais n'te promène donc pas toute nue!"* Ventroux's ambitions in his career as deputy are shaken, if not utterly destroyed, by his wife's nonchalance in walking about the house half-clad, and her utter naiveté in her relations with others. During a visit from her husband's political adversary, Clarisse is stung by a wasp and asks if someone won't save her life by sucking out the poison. The fact that she has been stung on the buttocks adds piquancy to the request.

Follavoine (*On purge bébé*) is likewise frustrated in his attempts to win a major contract. A manufacturer of porcelain, he hopes to get the contract to supply chamber pots to the entire French army. His shrewish wife, however, insults the representative from the Ministry, who goes seething out of the apartment, swearing to avenge his honor with a duel.

Feydeau's characters are harassed, restricted, limited, by their professions. Even more than the professional people, those who are civil servants, or who practice a humbler occupation, are seen in terms of their work. Employees of the city hall (*Occupe-toi d'Amélie, Le mariage de Barillon*), the courts (*L'Affaire Edouard*), and the police (*Monsieur chasse, L'Hôtel du Libre-Echange, Occupe-toi d'Amélie, La Main passe*) exercise little more than their civil function: judges are there to judge, mayors to marry, and police to arrest, or at least to witness adulterers caught red-handed. However briefly they appear, they are individualized. Suspicious, friendly, or gruff, they impress us as theatrical characters who fulfill their functions with personality as well as competence.

One of them, Amélie's father, Pochet, although retired, has not forgotten his former duties as traffic policeman. He continues now to use a comically official vocabulary bristling with malapropisms, and in moments of stress, attempts to direct the traffic through Amelie's apartment.

Although Feydeau most often centers his attention on the world of the well-to-do bourgeois, he includes people from all levels of society, from princes to peasants. One of the major characters in *La Duchesse des Folies-Bergère* is the young king of Orcanie, and he is surrounded by various members of the Orcanian aristocracy, including la Môme Crevette from *La Dame de chez Maxim*, now married to Baron Pitchenieff. The visiting Prince of Palestria comes to avail himself of the professional talents of Amélie in *Occupe-toi d'Amélie*, reflecting a *belle époque* reality.

Feydeau's only play which cannot be called a comedy, *Le Bourgeon*, is set chiefly in an aristocratic milieu, and stresses the class consciousness and bigotry of the landed nobility. *La Dame de chez Maxim*, in an entirely different key, takes us into an upper-crust salon in the provinces. There we see the affectations, hypocrisy and envy of provincial society aping the latest styles of Paris. Here, la Môme Crevette, masquerading as the wife of Dr. Petypon, is accepted as the model of the *dernier cri* in Parisian fashions. The stiff provincial ladies examine every detail of her dress, which would be considered vulgar and theatrical in the capital, and finally imitate her hip-swinging postures and ridiculous "fashionable" habit of throwing one leg over a chair and exclaiming, "C'est pas mon père!"—"It ain't my dad!"

In Feydeau's plays, the foolishness, bigotry, hypocrisy and selfishness of civilian society is matched by that of the military. A number of his characters go off to their 13 or 28 days of military duty, thereby setting off great complications. Champignol is particularly victimized by the military machine, as he loses every inch of hair.

Members of the military are seen as dehumanized; they function like machines and thus embody one of the classical forms of comic behavior. Sweeping all before them, they inflict the military code of obedience upon their often innocent victims. Champignol's uncle, mistaken for a recruit, is brutally mistreated, until his true identity is established, a comic and not too oblique commentary on the inhumanity of military life. Dr. Petypon (*La Dame de chez Maxim*), forced into a duel, is pushed aside by the seconds who discuss the weapons to be used and are deaf to his will in the matter. After all, he is only the duelist; etiquette and protocol are what matter.

The servants in Feydeau, maids and valets to settled bourgeois, or employees of dandies or *cocottes*, are invariably independent in spirit and often insolent. Rédillon's manservant, Gérôme (*Le Dindon*), who was with the family for years before becoming the young bachelor's valet, even uses the familiar "tu" form of speech with Rédillon, while the latter replies to him in the polite "vous" form. Sometimes extremely clever, the servants see their masters and mistresses with a critical eye, and are always aware of their shortcomings. Most insolent of them all, and but for a bit of bad luck the cleverest, is Justin in *Dormez, je le veux*.

His abilities as a hypnotist allow him to avoid all menial tasks, to dine at his master's table, and to escape the bothersome conversation of the master's family.

Some of the servants are innocents from the country, and they reveal their background by naive behavior and colorful language. Equally colorful, and sometimes just as naive, are the foreigners who are frequent visitors in *belle époque* Paris. They are a motley group, including Slavic princes, Latin American generals, American heiresses, English governesses, and Dutch or Belgian uncles, each speaking a savory French spiced with occasional foreign expressions, and mispronounced to comic effect. For some of his characters, particularly those from Eastern Europe, Feydeau has invented exotic languages which are vaguely familiar, yet incomprehensible. To help the actor intone correctly, he places the meaning in parentheses.

The foreigner who expresses himself inadequately finds himself at a disadvantage, but he is rarely the victim of his linguistic inability. There is, however, a group of characters in Feydeau's universe who, through some physical flaw or inexplicable deviation from natural behavior, express themselves in a manner which is somehow defective, indeed dehumanized. It is in *L'Hôtel du Libre-Echange* that we meet the first of these: Mathieu, a lawyer who has come to visit the Pinglets. Mathieu is troubled by stuttering whenever it rains, and when it storms, he is rendered speechless—thereby limiting his law practice to dry seasons.

Such a peculiarity is related to that of the accents and patois in other plays. But here there is something more fundamentally "wrong," a true deviation due not to national boundaries, but to something utterly beyond our comprehension. With the Spanish generals and

French peasants, communication may be difficult, but with Mathieu and his ilk, there is a total interruption. At once terribly comic, yet somehow pathetic in his inability to express himself, he is a victim of some strange force, some cruel destiny which seems to have singled him out for punishment.

Madame Pinchard, one of the clients in the Act II hotel of *Le Dindon*, is the reverse of Mathieu—where he cannot speak, she cannot hear. Both are incommunicado, but from different physical failings. The stone deaf old lady gives rise to many comic moments when she fails to understand her husband and replies nonsensically to his words. She can, however, read his lips so that, paradoxically, it is when we the audience cannot understand Pinchard's silently mouthed words that she understands him best. At one moment she complains bitterly that she cannot *see* what he is saying. As the apparently irrational turns out to be true, Feydeau brings us close to the edge of reason. A few decades later, Ionesco and others would push their characters over the brink.

One of the most riotously funny scenes in the play takes place when Mme Pinchard and her husband go to bed, thereby setting off the bells which were placed under their mattress by Pontagnac and Mme Vatelin (wife and would-be lover), a signal that the latter's husband has finally gone to bed with his English mistress. As a matter of fact, the room has been mistakenly assigned to two couples, and when the Pinchards go to bed, the husband, Vatelin, is out of the room and his English friend is in the bathroom. The poor deaf woman goes on blithely sleeping, while the entire hotel, in an uproar, invades her room, complaining of bells being rung in the middle of the night. In the midst of our hilarity, a note of nightmare is introduced as Mme Pinchard awakes to find herself surrounded by strangers. "What's the matter? What do you want?" she cries, and turns to her husband: "Pinchard, my love, there are some men after me!"

When all have finally gone, she remains imprisoned within her silent world, mystified by everything that has taken place. Kneeling on the bed, clutching a pillow as protection, she asks again, "What is the matter?" Pinchard, mingling a touch of tenderness and sympathy with a comic reflection on her total unawareness of what is going on about her, replies, "She didn't hear a thing! Well, Coco darling, you're the lucky one."

The last we see of her, she is running off after her husband, who is himself in hot pursuit of Vatelin whom, a moment before, he had discovered in his wife's bed. Her final words are anguished questions, reminding us again of the wordless world she inhabits where life "on the outside" is often meaningless. "Pinchard! Darling! Where are you going?"

Feydeau has transposed to a comic key the grating, ironic poetry of Tristan Corbière's "Rhapsody of the Deaf Man," but through the comedy pierce notes of personal tragedy.

Less tragic, because less credible, is the affliction of the stonemason Lapige in *La Main passe*. Born of a mother who had been frightened by a dog, Lapige barks when he becomes upset. His moments onstage are among the most hilarious in dramatic literature. Having found a suit of clothes on the sidewalk, Lapige has brought it to the address indicated in a pocket. The owner of the clothes, Massenay, has told his wife a fantastic tale to explain his appearance in borrowed clothes twice his size after having been gone all night. Angrily, he approaches Lapige and challenges him to assert that he, Massenay, was found anywhere near those clothes. All the mason can do is to hem and haw, then bark in the face of the astonished husband. "What?!" asks the unbelieving Massenay. "Woof! Woof!" replies Lapige.

A few minutes later, as he leaves the room, the police officer steps on his foot, and Lapige yelps like a wounded dog. His situation, at the limits of credibility, or rather beyond, falls patently into the absurd.

Farce in France has used the device of distorted speech since its beginnings. The masterpiece of medieval farce, *Pierre Pathelin,* delights us when the shepherd, coached by his lawyer Pathelin, replies to all the judge's questions with the "baaa!" of a bleating sheep. When Pathelin finally turns to him to collect his fees, the clever peasant continues to bleat. Voluntary animal noises to outwit those in power are one thing; however, Feydeau's afflicted have no choice—they outwit no one. Instead, it is they who suffer from the condition imposed upon them by their creator. When their afflictions are pushed beyond credibility, as in the case of Lapige, they are absurdity incarnate. Yet so relentless is the logic of Feydeau's world, that within that world we do not question their credibility.

Like Mme Pinchard, Camille, in *La Puce à l'oreille,* has a recognizable physical affliction which, nonetheless, renders him comical. Suffering from a cleft palate, he expresses himself almost exclusively in vowels, to the utter consternation and puzzlement of those who do not know him. Fortunately his defect can be corrected, and Dr. Finache has made him a silver palate. But in the catastrophes bound to overtake Feydeau's characters in the second act, Camille loses it.

Victims like Mathieu, Lapige, Mme Pinchard and Camille would, if we reflected, become frightening in their automatism, or pathetic in their suffering. Their plights offer us, on the level of physical suffering, a parallel to the victimization of most characters in the turbulent machinery of plot and action that carries them away with an irresistible force. Part of Feydeau's genius is to keep us balanced on that thin edge, on the verge of absurdity, but to write with such sedulous craftmanship and at such speed that we are never allowed a moment to reflect on the pathetic aspects of the afflicted.

Nightmare and the threat of an inimical universe remain a constant element in Feydeau's theater. They are reminders that, despite the hilarity and gaiety—and sometimes precisely because of them—we are never far removed from the heart of reality. The attention given to human suffering, physical inadequacies, bodily functions and the physiology of sex—not to mention the selfishness, egotism and materialism which dominate in Feydeau's disabused vision—justify a description of his *vaudevilles* as Naturalism seen in a comic perspective: a slice of life garnished with heaps of whipped cream and candied cherries.

A slice of life still seen in a comic light, but without the fruit and cream, is found in the plays of the other comic genius of the ending nineteenth century, Georges Courteline. Unlike Feydeau, Courteline was connected with theaters which espoused the cause of Naturalism. Already a journalist noted for his astute gift of observation and caustic commentary on the political and social institutions which overwhelmed and victimized the little man, he made his theatrical debut in 1891 at the Théâtre-Libre. His success there led to more performances in that bastion of Naturalism, and at Antoine's own Théâtre-Antoine which opened in 1897 with Courteline's masterly *Boubouroche*.

Courteline and Feydeau both satirize the institutions of marriage, the army, and the courts, and both reveal a basic truth in character and situation presented comically. But Courteline keeps his truth much closer to the surface, so that it is always apparent, even when the situation is aggravated. Treating only simple situations (all his plays but two are in a single act), Courteline never allows plot to overwhelm character, or structural violence to outstrip the picture of reality. Eschewing the metaphysical overtones suggested by Feydeau, Courteline is, like other Naturalist dramatists, fundamentally a writer of social plays. He shows us the ordinary citizen, the witless recruit, the naive lover or husband, and the unimaginative civil servant as victims of the law, the military, heartless women, or sadistic civil servants. Although his disabused optic seems to allow for no comforting solution to the dilemmas of most of his victims, Courteline views them with an indulgence that contrasts with Feydeau's more objective and cruel view.

Invariably mentioned in a single breath, and treated on adjoining pages in literary histories, Feydeau and Courteline are the outstanding comic writers of their day. When comparisons are made, it is not uncommon to find the balance inclining in favor of Courteline. Simplicity, realism and social awareness give him an air of seriousness which contrasts with Feydeau's apparent frivolity. Deep beneath that froth, however, there is more than an accidental resemblance to the realism of Courteline and other Naturalists.

The peak of Naturalism is represented in France by

two or three plays of Henry Becque, mordant, dispassionate critic of his contemporaries. One of the most popular was *La Parisienne* (1884; *Woman of Paris*), a love triangle in which Clotilde deceives not only her unsuspecting husband, but her jealous lover as well. Becque, having recently had *Les Corbeaux* (*The Vultures*) performed at the Comédie-Française, where it failed miserably, attempted in late 1884 to find a producer for *La Parisienne*. Curiously enough, it was through the insistence of Feydeau, then a young man known only for his gracious social monologues, that the manager of the Renaissance accepted the play. Feydeau, then secretary to the producer Samuel, particularly liked the opening scene of the play, and advised his employer to accept it. Becque, scornful of the author who was to write only "pitiful *vaudevilles*," could never forgive this young whippersnapper for having permitted himself to judge the work of a genius like himself.

Becque's vision of love and marriage is astonishingly similar to that of Feydeau, but reflects a more cruelly ironic perspective. Neither author gilds society, they present it as it is. If Becque's world is drab and strikes us as more "real" that is because he gives little importance to structure or rapidity of tempo, and does not exaggerate. Feydeau, on the other hand, beginning at a similar point pushes plot, character and situation until theatricality becomes apparent. The difference is one of proportion and not of intrinsic content.

The world of *La Parisienne* is one of cold, calculating women, blind, foolish husbands, and jealous, weak lovers. Becque's bourgeois, like Feydeau's, are vain, selfish and materialistic, using others to their own ends. Clotilde is a Francine (*La Main passe*) who has not yet been caught, and Lafont, the lover, finally convinced that she is betraying him, expresses in less vivid and lively language the thoughts shared by a number of Feydeau's hopeful lovers:

> In Paris you simply cannot keep a decent mistress, impossible! The more decent she is, the more difficult it is to keep her. . . . What am I going to do? If only Adolphe [Clotilde's husband] were here, we could spend the evening together. That's true: when I feel downhearted and Clotilde has upset me, I still feel best with her husband. I feel less alone. Adolphe's situation consoles me a little for my own; it's even worse than my own, certainly worse. . . . It's a sure thing, men are rarely happy; bachelor or cuckold, there's not much choice.
>
> (II, iv)

Played in the proper style, these words could be mistaken for those of Feydeau.

But the observant *vaudevilliste* does not stop at a picture of adultery and its comic consequences, although it is one of his major subjects. He reveals its causes as well. A number of plays show us the kind of marriage which leads to infidelity. Reading the late short plays, one can only be surprised that divorce was not more rapid. Thoughtless, selfish, shrewish wives parade through them taking advantage of their weak or witless husbands. The battle between the sexes is as relentless as the cruelest struggles in Strindberg, that mysogynist par excellence. Maligned, misunderstood, scorned, frustrated, the husbands in *On purge bébé* and *Hortense a dit: "Je m'en fous!"* finally, in utter exasperation, walk out. In *Feu la mère de madame* and *Léonie est en avance* they take a symbolic revenge, one by going off to sleep in his own bed, and the other by inverting a chamber pot on his father-in-law's head.

In these final masterful comedies of character, so different from the frothy *vaudevilles*, Feydeau shows himself the match of his realist contemporaries. But the disabused view of marriage was not new in 1908. The seeds of shrewishness are to be found in most of his wives, and the ironically named Angélique of *L'Hôtel du Libre-Echange* is a full-blown termagant as early as 1894. We can only sympathize with her husband, Pinglet, when he cries, "If only one could see a woman twenty years later, one would never marry her twenty years before!" At no matter what period of Feydeau's career, it seems safe to say: scratch a woman, you'll find a vixen.

Without adopting a tone of condemnation, in a completely dispassionate way, Feydeau sets next to such women husbands who are either faithless or cold. Pinglet's friend and neighbor, Paillardin, explains that he has no "temperament." As his wife Marcelle piquantly phrases it, "You can't expect a one-armed man to play the violin." Pinglet, on the other hand, has plenty of temperament, but cannot stand his wife—besides, he has been married twenty years. In drole imagery, he describes himself to Paillardin: "There's lava in me! Boiling hot lava! . . . But I just don't have a crater . . ." Paillardin, of course, never dreams that this volcano hopes to erupt with his wife. Pinglet himself hesitates, not out of friendship, but out of fear of failure: "After all I'm not the kind to play such a dirty trick on a friend—especially if I'm not sure of succeeding."

These can be dismissed as so many comic speeches, but they are more properly considered insights into the reality of marriage and sex. Sugaring the pill, Feydeau studies the state of conjugal morality in the Third Republic—or any time.

The self-righteousness and hypocrisy of the man on the make is both comedy and commentary when Pinglet cries out to Marcelle that he will not stand by and watch her being insulted by her neglectful husband, and in the name of French knighthood he immediately attempts to take her into his arms and declare his love. Similarly, comedy is heightened by truth when, a few minutes later his cross, curt wife, reading a prospectus for the obviously shady Hôtel du Libre-Echange which has arrived in the mail, comes across the line, "large discounts for subscriptions of twelve tickets." "Disgusting!" she exclaims. "Disgusting!" echoes Pinglet, and adds immediately under his breath, "I'll get twelve tickets."

The picture of love which emerges is that of an animal passion. Man, going after woman, has one thing in mind, and it is not spiritual union. We have already heard Rédillon, the young man who hopes someday to become Lucienne's lover in *Le Dindon*, reply to Lucienne's request that he kill the animal within him, that he cannot be cruel to animals. The wealthy bourgeois fattens his animal nature, devotes most of his time to it. When he is not seeking sexual pleasures, he may well be found sitting at a well-laden table. Eight or ten of the plays contain scenes in which tables prepared for dining grace the set, and at a number of them people are actually seated, dining. The bourgeois so grotesquely satirized by Jarry in *Ubu roi*, a creature devoted entirely to the baser appetites, is the same animal we see in Feydeau and Becque.

Grown tired of "leafing through the same book day after day," the faithless husband rushes headlong into what he hopes will be a thrilling sexual liaison. If he is fortunate enough to realize his wish—a rare occurrence in Feydeau, where wives only tease their lovers, lead them to the crucial moment, and then back down with protestations of innocence—the male of the species soon discovers that all women are alike, and that a mistress can become as tedious as a wife. The "morning after" bedroom conversation of Francine and Massenay (*La Main passe*) is every bit as vituperative and acrimonious as the most seasoned marital battle.

In *Le Dindon*, when Pontagnac follows Mme Vatelin from the street into her living room in a persistent attempt to have his way, she begins by preaching to him in a tone which reminds us of the more instructive pronouncements of the virtuous women who frequent the thesis plays of Dumas the younger and Emile Augier. Not one whit discouraged by this woman preacher, Pontagnac strives throughout the play to convince her of her husband's infidelity so that he may reap the rewards, only to discover at the final curtain that Lucienne really loves her husband, and forgives him his one lapse from conjugal fidelity—particularly since it happened in London and some years ago.

But Lucienne and Vatelin are unusual, for marital happiness is a rare commodity in this theater. The touching tone of the denouement is also rare in Feydeau's work, closer to a straight drama than to the gaiety of his usual manner. Like his single serious play, *Le Bourgeon*, it reminds us how closely Feydeau is related to the other authors of his day, and makes us grateful for his comic genius which saves him from sentimentality and gives his plays that cutting edge which all great drama possesses.

Le Dindon examines several forms of love: the

young couple, Lucienne-Vatelin; the old couple, Dr. and Mme Pinchard; and the one-night couple, Rédillon and his *cocotte*, Armandine. But it is in one of Feydeau's most popular plays, *La Puce à l'oreille*, that we find the most complete picture of love.

The flea placed in Raymonde's ear, and which rouses her suspicions, derives from her husband's recent sexual inadequacies. She describes her disappointment to her friend Lucienne:

> When for years a husband has been an impetuous torrent, and then suddenly, pfft! . . . nothing! dried up!
>
> (I, IV)

The husband, Chandebise, somewhat less graphic, takes a more psychological approach when he describes his difficulties to his friend, Dr. Finache:

> At first I wasn't too upset, strengthened by the memory of a glorious past. I told myself: after all, defeat today, revenge tomorrow! . . . But then the next day I had the unfortunate idea of telling myself: "Careful, old man! Let's don't let it happen again! . . ."
>
> (I, VIII)

Through what the doctor diagnoses as "autosuggestion" Chandebise has arrived at complete sexual impotence. The doctor's first surprised reaction is as anatomical— if not as appropriate—as Raymonde's description: "That's a bit stiff!" he exclaims.

When the already suspicious wife discovers that the suspenders she gave her husband as a gift have turned up at a shady hotel, she is convinced that he is guilty, and determines to set him a trap. Through a series of misunderstandings, instead of the husband, the family friend and her would-be lover, Tournel, turns up. Having convinced Raymonde that Chandebise is indeed faithless, Tournel believes he is about to realize his hopes as the wife's instrument of revenge. In a frenzy of passion, he covers Raymonde with kisses, and while she responds enthusiastically, she is actually exulting over her revenge rather than enjoying Tournel's embraces.

The difference in what Anouilh half a century later would call the two "races" of male and female, is sharply defined as Tournel presses his suit and attempts to pull Raymonde toward the bed, while the naive wife repulses him in shocked amazement:

> RAYMONDE: Are you crazy? What do you take me for?
> TOURNEL: What? But I thought you had agreed . . .
> RAYMONDE, *sharply and with great dignity*: To be your mistress, yes. But to go to bed with you! Ah! Do you think I'm a prostitute?
>
> (II, VI)

From opposite ends of the spectrum of love, they argue. Raymonde, innocently idealistic, claims that she is offering him "the best part of myself." "Which?" asks the frustrated lover. "My head . . . my heart," she replies. But Tournel turns up his nose at such treasures with a "pfu!", declaring he can hardly be satisfied with "the half of yourself . . . the least in keeping with the circumstances." Love in Feydeau's world, as in Becque's, is most often love in the broad French use of

that term, and not in the spiritualized sense which An-
glo-Saxons like to lend it. Of that love Raymonde's
friend Lucienne has had enough, and tells the former
that she would be overjoyed if her passionate Latin husband would become impotent and give her a rest.

Conjugal love and adultery are not the only forms of
love which fall under Feydeau's scrutiny in *La Puce à
l'oreille*. It is suggested that Dr. Finache has homosex-
ual proclivities, for he expresses disappointment when
he discovers that Ferraillon, the owner of the Hôtel du
Minet Galant, has fired his handsome hotel boy—who
was making inroads on the clients rather than doing his
work as bellboy.

The hotelkeeper himself, a former soldier, has a
notable sadistic penchant. His masochistic wife admir-
ingly tells him, "You beat so well!" And his new bellboy, Poche, once his subaltern in the army, derives his
own strangely masochistic pleasure from being kicked
in the pants by the commanding hotel proprietor. If
Poche strikes us as vaguely anal, the afflicted Camille,
who loses his corrective silver palate at the hotel, stands
(although unintentionally) for the other Freudian
type, the oral.

In an amusing scene, the alcoholic Poche, slightly
inebriated from the wine he has been snitching in the
cellar, is nonplussed by the behavior of Raymonde and
Tournel. The guilty pair in the hotel room believe that
the bellboy—a physical replica of Chandebise—is indeed Raymonde's husband. Falling on their knees to the
perplexed Poche, they beg him to take out his resent-
ments against them by beating them. Astonished,
Poche wonders whether all the world isn't sadomasochistic. His wonder, increasing when the lovely woman
asks him to kiss her as a sign of forgiveness, rises to its

zenith when Tournel makes the same request. In one cataclysmic scene the sexuality of the world is summed up with the lightest of touches.

Like all durable drama, Feydeau's masterpieces exist on several levels. Of most immediate appeal is that of comic situation and frenetic action, led at devilish speed by a supreme magician who is at every moment in complete control. It is this level which is often described by reviewers with such phrases as "fast and furious," or "a mad romp." It is the level of frivolity scornfully described by avant-gardist Antonin Artaud as digestive theater.

Beyond the digestive, however, there lies in Feydeau enough reality to give the perceptive viewer a good case of heartburn. The disillusioned picture of the social animal is not one to bring laughter to our lips. Yet, in an idiom anticipating that of moderns like Ionesco, Feydeau suggests sad truths in the gayest of manners.

Beyond the social commentary, only subtly suggested, lies a yet more modern level in Feydeau's works, which are indeed *mad* romps, fast and *furious*. At the edge of absurdity, the precise machinery of farce, set at this particular rhythm and in this particular context, suggests, as Artaud declares all theater was created to do, that "we are not free. And the sky can still fall on our heads."

Somewhat unexpectedly, the violence and absurdity of Feydeau, by their very excess, by their fury and madness, strike deeper than the apparently serious theater so vaunted by his contemporaries. Feydeau leads us to experience in our nerves what is only verbalized in much so-called serious theater.

The comic victim, caught in the cogs of an intricate mechanism from which there is no escape, has taken on a new meaning. How many of us, casting a glance at our world today, feel inclined to express the sentiments of almost all Feydeau's protagonists who, sooner or later, are led to exclaim, "My God! What a night!"

Insofar as Feydeau's is a theater which embodies its deepest meanings in its very structure, and through that awesome structure gives us a glimpse into the dizzying void of absurdity, he is the genial precursor of today's theater.

THE PLAYS

Tailleur pour dames, 1886
(*A Gown for His Mistress*)

Feydeau's first full-length play, and his first major triumph, was written while he was doing his military service. His experiences there are not reflected in the play, however, but were to turn up several years later in his next major success, *Champignol malgré lui.* The production date for *Tailleur pour dames* is usually given as 1887, but one of the finest Feydeau scholars and translators, Norman R. Shapiro, has established that the real date was 1886.

Although full-length, this three-act piece is still short when compared with Feydeau's major works. It is deserving of attention as his first success, and because it clearly shows the author's gift for enmeshing a number of plots and subplots into a complex mathematical construction. As in his other works, the *quiproquo*—scene of mistaken identity—is a major comic device which, at the same time, furthers the complicated plot.

Dr. Moulineaux, although married only six months, has just spent the night out, having forgotten his key

when he attended the Opera Ball in hopes of seeing a
female patient, Suzanne, whom he has not yet succeeded in seducing. Suzanne, however, was kept busy
by her own husband, and Moulineaux, returning home
in the early hours, found himself locked out and spent
the night on a bench. He attempts to excuse himself by
telling his wife, Yvonne, that he was at the bedside of a
very sick patient, Bassinet. In typical Feydeau fashion,
Bassinet is immediately announced and Moulineaux
finds himself in hot water, for Bassinet is extremely ob-
tuse and fails to understand the situation. The latter, although married, is wifeless, for he once left his wife for
five minutes on a bench in the Tuileries Gardens while
he went to light a cigar, and returned to see her running off with a soldier. In the geometric world of Feydeau, we can be sure she will turn up sooner or later
to complicate the lives of several characters. Bassinet,
who has an apartment for rent, has come to ask Moulineaux to recommend it to his patients. He generally
makes himself objectionable by his insistence and by
his penchant for telling stories.

Moulineaux's mother-in-law, Mme Aigreville, arrives, and Yvonne confides her suspicions regarding her
husband's infidelity. To prevent his mother-in-law
from talking with Bassinet, Moulineaux tells her he is
a patient with a very contagious disease, and in a comic
encounter Bassinet attempts to rent her an apartment,
while she makes every effort to keep him at a healthy
distance and recommends that he go back to bed. Mme
Aigreville does, however, promise to look at Bassinet's
apartment, since she refuses to stay under the same roof
with her profligate son-in-law.

Moulineaux has sent his valet, Etienne, to fetch his
dressing gown, but Etienne misunderstands and instead

of bringing the gown he puts it on (*la porter* instead of *l'apporter*), and ushers in the doctor's patient, Suzanne, who explains that she was unable to meet the doctor at the ball because her husband would not leave her. Moulineaux has decided to rent Bassinet's apartment, and asks Suzanne to meet him there. At this moment the husband, Monsieur Aubin, arrives, and seeing Etienne in dressing gown takes him for the doctor, handing his coat to Moulineaux who is wearing black coat and tie. Aubin attempts to consult Etienne regarding his health, and when he discovers he has made a mistake he stops Moulineaux and then Bassinet, trying to apologize to each for having handed him his coat. When Bassinet tries to tell him a story, Aubin escapes, leaving Bassinet with no one but the audience to hear his story. But as he begins, the orchestra cuts him short and the curtain falls.

The second act takes place in the apartment rented to Moulineaux by Bassinet. The former occupant was a dressmaker, and Bassinet has not yet had time to move out the mannequins and other materials she left behind. Into this setting Moulineaux brings Suzanne, who can only stay a moment since her husband is waiting downstairs. In fact, Aubin decides to come upstairs just as Moulineaux is kneeling and embracing Suzanne. Since Suzanne had told her husband she was having a dress fitting, he takes Moulineaux for the dressmaker, and believes him when he declares his name is M. Machin (Mr. Whatchamacallit). Aubin cannot stay long because he has an appointment with his own mistress, Rosa. Bassinet arrives, as do various clients of the former dressmaker, and finally Mme Aigreville who does not know that the apartment has already been rented. She is immediately suspicious of the situation,

Jacques Dacqmine and Madeleine Renaud in a scene from
Occupe-toi d'Amélie. The 1948 production directed by
Jean-Louis Barrault marks the beginning of Feydeau's
immense postwar popularity.

FEYDEAU ON THREE CONTINENTS
The universal appeal of Fedeau's farces is demonstrated by these photographs of productions here and abroad. Above, Tokyo's Shiki Theatrical Company in a tense moment from *La Puce à l'oreille*. Right above, Georges Vitaly's production of *La Puce* at the Théâtre Montparnasse in Paris. Right below, a scene from the Asolo State Theater Company production in Sarasota, Florida, with (l. to r. Sharon Spelman, Bradford Wallace, and Patrick Egan).

FEYDEAU IN FRANCE

Above, "the Sun King" comes home from the Four Arts Ball in the Centre Dramatique du Nord production of *Feu la mère de madame*. Right above, the morning before the night after in Paris' Théâtre Marigny production of *L'Hôtel du Libre-Echange*. Right below, Madeleine Renaud starred in *"Mais n'te promène donc pas toute nue!"* at the Théâtre de l'Odéon, the Comédie-Française's "second theater."

FEYDEAU: ALWAYS IN SEASON
Left, at the Théâtre Antoine, Micheline Presle stars in
La Main passe. The men in her life are Jean Brochard,
André Luguet, and Bernard Lajarrige. Below, a scene
from the same play presented as *Chemin de fer* at the
Center Theatre Group-Mark Taper Forum, Los Angeles.
The barking bricklayer returns Fédot's clothes. From left

to right, Jack Dodson, Eric Christmas, Joan Van Ark, and Peter Church. Top right, a scene from *Le Dindon* as given at the Comédie-Française with Robert Hirsch, Jacques Charon, Yvonne Gaudeau, Gisèle Casadesus, and Jean Meyer. Bottom right, Lucette discovers an impressive ring in a bouquet from an admirer in the Comédie-Française production of *Un Fil à la patte*.

Michael O'Sullivan (left) and Herman Poppe in Gower Champion's all black-and-white production of *A Flea in Her Ear* for San Francisco's American Conservatory Theatre. The production was also seen in New York.

but Moulineaux claims he is visiting a patient, and when M. Aubin returns, he hastily pushes Suzanne and his mother-in-law into the next room and follows them, leaving Bassinet to cope with Aubin. Aubin takes Bassinet for the doctor, and is mightily impressed when he is told that the dressmaker is busy in consultation with the Queen of Greenland. When Mme Aigreville sails through the room on her way out, he bows and scrapes and calls her "Highness."

Aubin has recommended the dressmaker to his mistress, Rosa, and she now arrives carrying her little dog. She sends Aubin to walk the dog, and then chats over old times with Moulineaux, whom she has recognized as an old acquaintance. She tells him how she had married, but had left her husband who had gone off to light a cigar, leaving her sitting on a bench in the Tuileries. Suzanne, tried of waiting, bursts into the room and accuses Rosa of being Moulineaux's mistress. Rosa claims that her husband is just downstairs, and when Aubin returns, she introduces him as her husband. Suzanne (Mme Aubin), furious at this betrayal, goes off swearing revenge. Aubin runs after her, and Rosa swoons into Moulineaux's arms just as Yvonne arrives, intending to meet her mother in order to inspect the apartment. Seeing this proof of her husband's infidelity, she rushes off, followed closely by Moulineaux, who hands the inert Rosa over to the newly arrived Bassinet. Recognizing his long lost wife, he kisses her, she wakes, cries out "My husband!" and gives him a resounding slap as the curtain falls.

Back at Moulineaux's home, the distraught doctor is waiting for his wife, who has not returned home since the day before. Aubin arrives in the same predicament, followed soon by Yvonne and Mme Aigreville. Moul-

ineaux convinces his wife that the two women at Bassinet's apartment were the wife and mistress of Aubin,
and that he himself was only there as a doctor in consultation. Aubin, watching the scene of reconciliation,
believes that M. Machin (the lady's tailor, in reality
Moulineaux) is the lover of Bassinet's wife, for he takes
Bassinet to be the doctor. Aubin almost compromises
matters by inquiring about M. Machin's dresses, and he
is further astounded, when Bassinet arrives, to see the
latter watch calmly while Moulineaux speaks tender
words to Yvonne.

Aubin, who hopes to meet his wife at the hour when
she usually comes for her "medical consultation" with
Moulineaux, asks the latter to please tell her that Rosa
is his (the doctor's) mistress. Moulineaux refuses, and
finally Bassinet is prevailed upon to make the false admission, although he does not know that they are talking about his own wife. To make things look more
convincing, Aubin hands him a photograph of Rosa,
but he does not have time to look at it before Suzanne
enters. Almost immediately Rosa arrives, and both
Moulineaux and Aubin attempt to silence her and get
her out of the way, while the women turn on their
heels and refuse to meet her, each believing her to be
the mistress of her husband. Finally all is cleared up
when Bassinet introduces her as his wife. Aubin attempts to retrieve the photograph, but Bassinet looks at
it, notes the resemblance of Aubin's mistress to his own
wife, but finally convinces himself that it is really totally unlike Rosa.

The comedy of misunderstanding underlies the plot
of *Tailleur pour dames*, and is used in a variety of ways.
It is amplified by other traditional comic devices:
names (Mme Aigreville means Mrs. Bitterville), the in-

TAILLEUR POUR DAMES | 89

version of master for servant (Etienne is the first of many insolent valets—he not only wears his master's dressing gown but gives him advice and even speaks of the possibility of sleeping in his master's bed). The physical comedy of farce is everywhere evident, and most remarkably in an amusing scene where Bassinet nervously buttons up Aubin's overcoat, which Aubin immediately unbuttons. The patently absurd is accepted as credible: Aubin complains of bad circulation to Bassinet, whom he believes to be the doctor. Bassinet recommends he get a masseur, strip him and massage him for an hour. "Oh, I always went about it backwards," says the patient, grateful for the advice.

While Feydeau does not hesitate at asides or remarks made directly to the audience by his characters, *Tailleur pour dames* is the only play in which he uses the theatricalist device, not infrequent in music hall or forms of entertainment less structured than drama, of having the theater orchestra drown out the words of a character as the curtain falls.

The comic device of repetition underlines the embarrassment of the first of many scenes in Feydeau's plays showing a nervous lover about to enjoy his mistress for the first time. As Moulineaux hopes to take Suzanne into his arms in his newly rented love nest, she tells him that her husband is waiting downstairs—an idea which considerably cools his ardor. He can only murmur, "Ah, what a dear Suzanne!" The woman, as usual more self-possessed than the male, points out that he is repeating himself.

Suzanne is the first of those irritating women who, while enjoying adultery (or hoping to), constantly protest their innocence. Her morals are no higher than Moulineaux's. The doctor, arriving first for the rendezvous, admits "I've got a guilty conscience. But I won't listen to it." Suzanne is afraid someone might come and see them, because, "If someone saw us . . . I would be guilty." Secret sins don't count.

Although it was Feydeau's first success, *Tailleur pour dames* has not often been revived. Quite recently, however, it has made its appearance on television. Lacking the bite and violence which give depth to Feydeau's later masterpieces, this highly amusing *vaudeville*, through its one-dimensional characters, scarcely begins to suggest the oblique social commentary we witness in later Feydeau. Even less does it intimate the cruelty of an absurd universe.

Monsieur chasse, 1892
(*The Happy Hunter* or
13 Rue de l'Amour)

This three-act play, along with *Champignol malgré lui,* marks the beginning of Feydeau's long series of successes. The two plays were written after a year or two of silence, during which Feydeau studied the methods and techniques of the masters of *vaudeville* and farce, and incorporated what he had learned into his new works. *Monsieur chasse* was readily accepted by the director of the Palais-Royal, thus encouraging the young author, who had become disheartened by the lukewarm successes his plays had received over the past few years. With *Monsieur chasse* we find the same spirited Feydeau of the earlier plays, but he has gained breadth and vigor, and appears to have found the theme which was to become his province: adultery, and most particularly the unfaithful husband whose behavior, once discovered, gives rise to a desire for revenge on the part of the wife.

Léontine, with her husband's friend (and her own would-be lover), Moricet, is making up cartridges for

her husband, Duchotel, who is about to leave on one
of his frequent hunting trips down to the estate of his
friend, Cassagne. Moricet is indignant at Léontine's re-
fusal to give in to him and reminds her of the tender
hug she gave him when he shared her grief at the death
of her pet bird some months ago. He took this as a tacit
promise, but Léontine, preparing the further complications in the intrigue, tells him that as long as she knows
her husband is faithful, she will remain faithful. But
if she ever learns that he is having a liaison, she will go
to Moricet and say, "Avenge me!"

Moricet, without malice, sows a bit of doubt in
Léontine's mind by telling her some husbands use the
pretext of going hunting in order to go off and see a
mistress. He also notes that recently, when bringing
home his catch, Léontine's husband has brought hares
and rabbits together, whereas it is known that hares
and rabbits do not frequent the same areas. When
Duchotel enters, Moricet temporarily leaves, and Léontine confronts him with the facts about hares and rabbits, but he is unruffled and successfully explains that he
goes hunting in two different areas.

Duchotel goes off to try on some new clothes he has
just had made, copies of the stylish clothing of his
nephew Gontran, leaving Moricet to leaf through a volume of poetry of his own composition which he had
given to Duchotel, and which the latter had simply
used to prop up the short leg of a table. While he re-
reads his own verse with obvious pleasure, Moricet is
interrupted by the arrival of Gontran, Duchotel's
nephew, a schoolboy who is having his first affair—
with an older *cocotte*. Gontran has come to get from
his uncle some money to spend on the woman. He
sends her a telegram, and when the maid reads the

address aloud we recognize the same address as that of Moricet's new bachelor apartment.

Duchotel now appears and writes a telegram to his friend Cassagne to announce his imminent arrival, but in reality he is writing to Mme Cassagne, with whom he is having an affair. Her address is the same as the mistress of Gontran and Moricet. Having tricked his uncle into giving him 500 francs, Gontran runs off and Duchotel soon leaves to take his "train to the country." No sooner has he left than the maid introduces a man who has been waiting in the salon: Monsieur Cassagne! Léontine recognizes her husband's deceit when Cassagne tells her he has not seen Duchotel for six months, and that he has never been a hunter. She is furious and vows revenge, not even listening to Cassagne's announcement that he has at last found the occasion to catch his wife in *flagrante delicto*, since she is to meet her lover tonight. He intends to be there with the police and thus finally be able to divorce her.

The second act is classic Feydeau: all hell breaks loose as everyone who should not meet comes into collision. At 40 rue d'Athènes, we are in Moricet's bachelor quarters, formerly occupied by Gontran's *cocotte* who has been ousted without the schoolboy's knowledge, although he still has his personal key to the door. Across the hall on the same floor is the apartment of Mme Cassagne. Thus in one building live (or are assumed to live) three people who are involved in the lives of the characters of Act I, and during the course of Act II, all the major characters of the first act credibly turn up at 40 rue d'Athènes.

The first of a number of delightful character roles in Feydeau is that of the former aristocrat, Mme Latour. She has now fallen on evil days and become a con-

cierge as the result of her husband's discovery of her
penchant for falling in love with lion tamers and such.
Mme Latour is arranging Moricet's apartment when
Duchotel arrives looking for Mme Cassagne. Mme Latour is about to take him across the hall and let him into
the apartment to await the return of his mistress, according to instructions, when they are interrupted by
the arrival of Moricet and Léontine, the latter now
ready to give herself to Moricet in order to avenge herself on her husband. Mme Latour pushes Duchotel into
a closet, gets the illicit couple into the next room,
then sends Duchotel off to wait for his married mistress in her apartment.

Left alone with Léontine, Moricet attempts to make
love to her, but she is reticent, until he reminds her that
at this very moment her husband is somewhere making
love to Mme Cassagne. The concierge returns to help
them locate some champagne for their dinner, and
while Moricet is searching for it in an adjoining room,
Mme Latour mentions her own misfortunes to Léontine, who begins to wonder whether she is not making
a mistake. Furthermore, the fallen aristocrat claims that
when a man says he is going hunting, that is a sign that
he does not trust his wife, and is setting a trap for her.
Léontine, in a panic, insists upon leaving, but Moricet
will not hear of it. Furious, she says she will spend the
night on the sofa, and finally goes off with a cover to
sleep on a chaise longue in the next room. Mme Latour
arrives with a message from a neighbor who has had an
attack of nerves and wishes Moricet, who is a doctor,
to treat her. He refuses, and Duchotel himself comes to
beg him to help. When he discovers his friend, Moricet, he is curious to know who his woman friend is.
Moricet, at random, picks the name of Mme Cassagne,

but Duchotel of course realizes it is a lie. Léontine now tries to enter, but Moricet has locked the door and in order to muffle her angry shouts, lest her husband recognize the voice, he sings at the top of his lungs the final trio from *Faust*, soon joined by Duchotel.

When he is rid of Duchotel, Moricet unlocks the door, but not wishing to compromise Duchotel he only tells Léontine to remain hidden—her honor depends upon it—and then rushes off to treat the neighbor, Mme Cassagne. Duchotel returns just as Léontine enters the room. She recognizes him but has time to cover herself with a blanket before her husband is aware of her presence. Moricet returns, having taken care of Mme Cassagne, and when Duchotel goes off, the two settle down for the night once again, Moricet in his bed onstage, and Léontine, in a rage, in the adjoining room.

Into the darkened room comes Gontran, having let himself in with his personal key. He jumps into bed with the sleeping Moricet and tries to embrace him, and Moricet thinks it is Léontine, who has finally given in and come to bed. Gontran assumes that Moricet is the old man who is keeping his *cocotte*, and he hides in a closet, while Léontine, wakened by the noise, convinces Moricet that he has simply had a nightmare. At this moment the police arrive, having taken the wrong turn in the corridor, and they attempt to arrest Moricet and Léontine, thinking that they are Mme Cassagne and her lover. Moricet finally sets the police commissioner aright and sends him across the hall, and then follows Léontine into the next room to try to calm her. Through the window, which opens onto a balcony running around the entire building, we see Duchotel enter, carrying his hunting gun, and dressed in hasty fashion in all but his pants. Seeing Moricet's trousers on a chair, he puts them on and flees, but not without having glimpsed and been glimpsed by Gontran who, at that moment, was attempting to escape from his closet. Two policemen enter quickly through the window, looking for the guilty lover who fled without his pants. Moricet, hearing them, enters pantless, and is taken off by the police, while Léontine stands by helpless, then flees as Gontran once again comes out of his closet and recognizes his aunt.

In the final act, the following morning, Léontine is exasperated with Moricet for not having had the forethought to keep his pants more carefully guarded, for in one pocket was her letter to him asking him to avenge her. Now her husband is in possession of both pants and letter. Duchotel arrives with his "catch" from hunting, and makes up a fantastic story of his hunt with Cassagne. When Léontine opens the "catch" she finds canned pâté, for the grocer had misunderstood Duchotel. In the face of such a gaffe, and his wife's meeting with Cassagne, Duchotel lies boldly and inventively, telling Léontine that Cassagne had a sunstroke in Africa and has totally lost his memory. If only he were here now: at which point he enters, and makes matters even worse, for he understands the situation not at all. He is delighted to have caught his wife with her lover, a certain Moricet, and asks Duchotel if he knows him. Not at all, claims the latter, at which point Moricet is announced, and Duchotel introduces him as his shirtmaker, which leads to a scene of mistaken assumptions and confused identities.

Moricet gets his pants back from Duchotel, who refuses, however, to accept the responsibility for Mme Cassagne's adultery, and insists that Moricet take the rap. Gontran's arrival puts everyone in a tizzy, for he has seen them all at 40 rue d'Athènes. To silence him they each offer him, in asides, gifts of money, and tell him to wait in the salon. The police commissioner arrives, bearing as evidence the pants of the guilty lover who fled the night before. Duchotel is almost forced to admit they are his, when Gontran, tired of waiting, comes in and innocently recognizes his pants—for the uncle had copied his nephew's stylish clothes.

While Duchotel shows the commissioner out, Léontine and Moricet frantically and vainly search for her letter in the pants he has retrieved. Now, despite her irritation at her husband's guilt, Léontine's own guilt will be apparent if Duchotel finds the letter. When he enters, he does indeed find the letter in his pocket, but in his blindness and vanity, he believes it is an old letter Léontine had written him at the time of their engagement, and he asks her to forgive him in memory of that happy time. She resists, until Gontran asks her in an aside to forgive her husband in the name of the lady he saw at 40 rue d'Athènes the night before. As the curtain falls, all is pardoned and Duchotel promises never to hunt again.

This simplified recounting of the plot makes apparent the complexity and tightly-woven interrelationships which make this play (and those that follow) different from Feydeau's earlier works. It is a matter of degree, for here the earlier complexities are aggravated, and the various strands are woven together much more closely in a way which is immensely satisfying. Coincidence is rife, and the amusing announcement of a character's arrival almost immediately after its impossibility or unadvisability has been made clear, is used three times to great comic effect, but each time with a variant. It is apparent that Feydeau has now formulated his famous rule of bringing together as quickly as possible people who had best not meet.

Quiproquo is used a number of times as are the other standard comic devices of farce: slapstick, important objects, the classic cupboard, and for the first time—but not the last in Feydeau's long career—a man is caught without his pants.

A new awareness of rhythm, pace, and the importance of the physical movement of characters and objects is apparent, as Feydeau becomes more sure of himself. For the first time he gives precise stage directions, describes details of the setting, and insists upon certain effects and special ways of interpretation. The plays gain in intensity and energy, accenting the puppet-like behavior of men, victims of the whirlwind forces their lies and mistakes set loose.

It is with *Monsieur chasse* that we begin to feel, however slightly and benignly, Feydeau's critical observation of the bourgeois and of marriage. Lies, hypocrisy, and a fatuous self-righteousness characterize the male, while the woman is quick to leap to her revenge, but never quite ready to live up to the bargain she has made. Léontine backs away at the sight of Moricet's bed, and when she finally allows him to kiss her, she is enjoying her revenge rather than her romance. The intended night of love ends in anger and recriminations. Ultimately, all Feydeau's characters are prisoners of their own selfish world, but the dramatist makes merry with that egotism and uses it to reveal their comic automatism.

The Act III scene in which Gontran embarrasses Duchotel, Moricet and Léontine, each of whom is afraid he will reveal to the others his (or her) presence at 40 rue d'Athènes, offers a foretaste of the theater of

the absurd. It is almost pure Ionesco. Standing in a row
across the stage, they know not what to say:

> DUCHOTEL, *after a moment, as though someone
> had spoken to him*: What?
> LÉONTINE, *surprised and smiling*: Nothing.
> DUCHOTEL: Ah!
> MORICET: No!
> DUCHOTEL: I thought. *Eyes ceilingward, breathing
> noisily*. Pffu!
> LÉONTINE: Pffu!
> MORICET: Pffu!

(III, x)

A few moments later, having gotten rid of Gontran,
they are threatened by a new contretemps as the doorbell rings. Like the characters in Ionesco's *La Cantatrice chauve* (*The Bald Soprano*), but more human and
within a complicated situation, they react:

> DUCHOTEL, *pulling himself together, and adopting
> a playful tone in order to deceive his wife, but
> fooling no one*: Someone . . . someone rang.
> LÉONTINE, *for the same reasons as her husband,
> with little affirmative shakes of her head and a
> forced smile*: Someone rang, yes, yes.
> MORICET, *the fifth wheel*: Someone . . . someone
> rang!
> *A pause.*
> DUCHOTEL, *same business*: Who could it be?
> LÉONTINE, *same business, spreading her arms wide
> to express ignorance*: Ah!
> MORICET, *same business*: Neither do I!

(III, x)

Monsieur chasse was understandably an immediate
success. Although not one of Feydeau's most famous

plays today, it has been revived almost regularly at 15 to 20 year intervals in France. It was, so far as is known, the first Feydeau play to be performed in New York, having had a presentation there in the 1890s. More recently it was performed, as the American première, in Illinois, under the title *13 rue de l'Amour*. Yet a third American première was announced in 1972, when the Dallas Theatre Center performed *The Happy Hunter*.

Champignol malgré lui, 1892
(Champignol in Spite of Himself)

Along with *Monsieur chasse*, this play marks the beginning of Feydeau's uninterrupted series of successes. It enjoyed 422 performances—triple that of *Monsieur chasse*, which, it will be remembered, the manager of the Palais-Royal had preferred to it. Francisque Sarcey, dean of drama critics of his day, declared that "at the end of the play, the hysterical laughter that had taken over and was shaking the entire audience was so noisy that the actors could no longer be heard, and the act ended in pantomime."

Lickety-split, *Champignol malgré lui* moves from one absurdity to another, accumulating momentum as it goes, and exploding into a series of hilarious situations. As the curtain rises we are plunged into a favorite Feydeau situation: the lover intent upon seducing a married woman. During the absence of Angèle's famous painter husband, Champignol, her would-be lover, Saint-Florimond, comes into her apartment in an attempt to seduce her. All is over, she declares, and asks him to leave. She is, moreover, irritated at his lack of foresight, for not long ago she had, in a moment of weakness, consented to spend two days with him in Fontainebleau. He had chosen, quite by chance, the same hotel in which Angèle's Swiss uncle and his daughter and son-in-law were staying. They had assumed that the man with Angèle was her husband. The same assumption is made by the new maid, Charlotte, a country bumpkin, when she comes into the room and discovers Saint-Florimond giving Angèle a farewell kiss.

As Saint-Florimond attempts to leave he meets on the stairs the Swiss uncle, Chamel, with his daughter and son-in-law. Passing through Paris, they have stopped for a brief visit, thus making Saint-Florimond's departure impossible. The son-in-law, Singleton, is on his way to Clermont, where he must do his military service. The family is interrupted by the arrival of Camaret, captain of the 175th regiment in Clermont, accompanied by his daughter Adrienne and her cousin Célestin. Chamel and family recognize Camaret as the man who is to command Singleton during his military duty, and they ask his benevolence. Camaret, whose daughter will soon be married, has come to ask Champignol to paint her portrait.

No sooner have the guests left than the police arrive to arrest Champignol, who is three days late in showing up for his military service—he, too, in Clermont. Since the maid assures them that Saint-Florimond is Champignol, they carry him off, and Angèle goes after him to try to save the situation in Clermont.

Champignol himself returns home to find the house almost empty. The servant Joseph, who has been out on errands and has not witnessed the abduction of

Saint-Florimond, reminds his master that he is three days late for his military service, and as the curtain falls Champignol too hurries off to Clermont where, although he does not know it, all the other characters of the play have rendezvous.

To the domestic madness of Act I, Act II adds military madness, as the major characters whirl in and out of the barracks setting at Clermont. Indeed, one is tempted to see in this act, however lightly etched, a commentary on the folly and inhumanity of the military, which Feydeau knew firsthand, having done his own military service. The impersonality and danger of a machine gone mad forms a double-edged instrument, cutting human freedom and individuality with one blade, and carving scenes of trenchant satire with the other.

The green recruits are severely criticized by their sergeant, and Singleton assures his companions that when his friend, Captain Camaret, arrives, he will set things right. But Camaret does not even recognize the young man, much less recall his promise of benignity, and assigns him two days of special duty as punishment for his familiarity.

When the recruits have been sent off to get uniforms, Angèle arrives and asks, as a special favor of Camaret, permission to see her "husband," Saint-Florimond-Champignol, who has been put in military jail for having missed his first three days of service. When alone with him, she asks him to do all 13 days of her husband's service, so that Champignol will not have to become involved in the already complicated events. Saint-Florimond promises, and expresses his need to get free for the evening, in order to attend a ball given by a Mme Rivolet, who lives in the environs. This is an

appointment he had made before becoming entangled
in Champignol's military service, and it was to serve to
introduce him to a wealthy young lady who might
well become his fiancée.

As Saint-Florimond goes back to his prison duty, the
real Champignol arrives, wearing his uniform, and carrying his painting equipment. Lieutenant Ledoux, who
has not yet laid eyes on Saint-Florimond, takes the new
arrival for the already-imprisoned Champignol, and in
the following scenes complications arise when orders
are given regarding one Champignol and carried out on
the other.

During the military exercises, Chamel and his daughter Mauricette watch from the terrace of the nearby
hotel, and are mortified at the treatment Singleton receives at the hands of Camaret. Chamel intends to go
fishing, while Mauricette goes off to see Mme Rivolet,
to whom they have received an introduction from the
prefect of their canton. Camaret orders Champignol
to be brought in, and asks Saint-Florimond-Champignol
to paint his portrait. For a time, Saint-Florimond resists, saying he has no equipment, but a soldier finds
the real Champignol's painting equipment in the barracks, and Saint-Florimond is forced to make an attempt at painting the captain. The real Champignol,
doing clean-up duty, passes by and attempts to criti-
cize Saint-Florimond's efforts, but is sent away angrily
by the captain. When the painting session is over, Camaret notices that Saint-Florimond's hair is too long and
orders Ledoux to have Champignol's hair cut. Ledoux
sends the real Champignol to the barber, and the next
time Camaret sees Saint-Florimond he orders Ledoux
to carry out his orders immediately. Again the real
Champignol receives a haircut. This happens a number

of times until Champignol is utterly bald, and Camaret, annoyed at the individualist hairstyle of this recruit— whom he, of course, does not know to be Champignol —condemns him to extra punishment. He also metes out punishment to Ledoux for not carrying out his orders, and Ledoux passes the punishment on down the line until Champignol gets it in the neck from everyone.

In the meantime, Chamel has fallen into the river, and while his clothes are drying he is given a uniform to wear. The commander of the post takes him for a soldier, orders him punished for lack of courtesy to an officer, and the phlegmatic Swiss is briefly caught up in the nightmare military life—until Singleton brings back his dry clothes, and it is recognized that he is not a soldier after all.

Ledoux orders Sergeant Belouette to have Champignol do guard duty that evening, and Belouette goes off to send Saint-Florimond-Champignol, while Ledoux encounters the real Champignol and tells him he is to do guard duty. In the long-awaited scene in which the two Champignols meet, the two guards become friendly and perform their duty walking arm in arm. Saint-Florimond reveals to Champignol his peculiar situation, but the naive husband does not suspect he is the man being replaced by his interlocutor. When Saint-Florimond discovers his companion's identity he almost passes out, gives a false name for himself, and invents another for the painter he is replacing.

Camaret and his nephew Célestin arrive, and Saint-Florimond is sent back to jail. Camaret we now learn is the brother of Mme Rivolet, and Célestin is her son. It is at his home that Saint-Florimond is to be introduced to his fiancée, Adrienne, whom he has already met in Act I in his identity as Champignol. Angèle learns these facts, and asks once more to see her husband, since she must warn Saint-Florimond not to go to the ball. Camaret orders Ledoux to send Champignol to his wife, and Ledoux of course sends the real Champignol. When he kisses her and takes his wife off to her hotel, the soldiers who have now arrived believe that Saint-Florimond-Champignol's wife is cuckolding him with another recruit. The story is too good not to tell, and when the real Champignol comes out of the hotel, newly-arrived soldiers who had not seen him go off with Angèle tell him of the cuckolding of Champignol. He now realizes *he* is the painter Saint-Florimond was talking about, and as the latter dashes off to Mme Rivolet's ball, Champignol is thrust into prison, the real Champignol now replacing the false one.

At Mme Rivolet's home, Adrienne is crushed that her cousin Célestin has not made an effort to stop the ball and the consequent meeting with her suitor, Saint-Florimond. It is only now that she realizes that Célestin really loves her, and the two of them vow to marry despite all plans. Adrienne's father, Camaret, is only too happy to do anything for his daughter's happiness.

When Saint-Florimond arrives, Camaret sees him, and asks why he is not in prison. He claims he is not Champignol, and so Camaret sends back to the post an order to send Champignol. In due time the real Champignol arrives and is reconciled with his wife, who convinces him that she is innocent and that she had caused Saint-Florimond to replace him for his reserve duty in order to save him from punishment. Champignol determines to punish Saint-Florimond for his attempted seduction, and when Camaret confronts the two, the real Champignol insists that he is Saint-Florimond and therefore not supposed to be a soldier at all; poor Saint-Florimond is forced to accept his role as Champignol. As the curtain falls, Camaret orders once again that his hair be cut.

One can see why a not too imaginative theater manager might have thought such a play condemned to failure. In a sense that judgment is a measure of its originality. The texture of improbabilities, coincidences and absurdities must have struck him as too difficult to swallow.

Champignol is the first of Feydeau's truly extravagant concoctions in which not one of the complications is superfluous. The masterly exposition leads through madness to a deeply satisfying denouement in which every apparently unrelated element falls neatly into place, and Saint-Florimond receives the punishment he deserves.

Many of the typical *vaudeville* effects are used, but they are often pushed almost beyond absurdity. In the opening scene, Saint-Florimond, attempting to enter Angèle's bedroom, speaks in falsetto hoping she will believe it is her chambermaid. The peasant accent of the new maid, and the Swiss accent of Chamel are used to comic effect, as is the ever-present *quiproquo*, here raised to the nth degree in the second act as Champignol is gradually shorn of his hair. As so often happens, the mistaken identity underlies the entire plot, but here, for once, it is not cleared up at the end.

We are occasionally given a foretaste of the masterly characterizations of Feydeau's later plays. They are only glimpses, and as always they are bathed in a comic light, as when Angèle rejects Saint-Florimond's advances, saying, "What! Deceive my husband! One of the most famous painters of our day!"

Despite such flashes, commentary on marriage and morals is held to a minimum, while the satire of military life reaches a paroxysm.

Champignol's appeal lies in its excess, and in our age of excesses it lies waiting to be rediscovered. Often revived from 1892 to 1930, since then it has only been rarely performed, and is not at present in print in an English version. At the threshold of Feydeau's mature career, it stands, in the words of Antoine, founder of the Naturalist-oriented Théâtre-Libre, as "an enormous success which was to remain a legend."

Un Fil à la patte, 1894
(*Cat Among the Pigeons*
or *Not by Bed Alone*)

This is one of Feydeau's masterpieces, incorporating all the techniques which are peculiar to his genius within an insanely fast-paced, carefully logical plot. It concerns the efforts of Bois-d'Enghien to break off with his mistress, Lucette, in order to marry. But since he has *un fil à la patte*, or is tied to her by the leg, he experiences peculiar and hysterical difficulties in making the break. This is the first full-length play whose principal female role is that of a *cocotte* instead of the wife, who has been standard until now.

Lucette, a famous popular singer, is sleeping late since her lover, Bois-d'Enghien, apparently ill for several weeks, has just returned to her and she is overjoyed. Friends and family (her old maid sister, her former husband, a *cocotte*, and a friend whose bad breath is a constant nuisance) are kept waiting for lunch, but are happy that Lucette's great love has returned. It transpires that, in fact, Bois-d'Enghien had come to break off, but had not had the courage to do so. Each time that he is about to bring up the subject of his forthcoming marriage Lucette kisses him or says something affectionate and he is unable to continue.

In the same issue of *Le Figaro* that announces Bois-d'Enghien's marriage, there is a laudatory review of Lucette's singing, so all her friends bring copies of the paper to her. Bois-d'Enghien spends a good deal of his time grabbing papers and stuffing them into his smoking jacket and pockets so that Lucette will not read about his marriage.

While the company is eating, the Baroness, who is to become Bois-d'Enghien's mother-in-law, arrives, hoping to engage Lucette to sing at the contract signing party that evening. At the same time, Bouzin, a foolish and untalented songwriter comes to see what Lucette's reaction has been to a song he recently left for her. Finding a magnificent bouquet left by some anonymous admirer, he decides to hide his own calling card in it and thereby get credit for the regal gift. The butler returns Bouzin's song with unflattering comments and he leaves in a huff, soon followed by the Baroness who plans to return later to engage the singer for the evening.

Lucette, finding Bouzin's card in the bouquet, and then a magnificent ring hidden near it, decides that she has made an error in assaying Bouzin's potential, and when the songwriter returns for his forgotten umbrella, everyone treats him with great deference and offers him a chair to sit in. Bois-d'Enghien hopes that Bouzin will take Lucette off his hands. After Bouzin has left to fetch his song once more, General Irrigua, a passionate, violent and jealous Latin American, makes his appearance. It soon becomes apparent that he is responsible for bouquet and ring. Since he loudly proclaims his intention to kill anyone who comes between him and Lucette, Bois-d'Enghien, in order not to endanger his own life, tells him that Bouzin is Lucette's lover. Bouzin returns with his song, the General attacks him furiously, but Lucette, realizing his lies about the bouquet, throws the songwriter out.

At the Baroness' home we discover her daughter, Viviane, is scarcely thrilled with the prospect of marrying Bois-d'Enghien, for she believes he is pure and chaste, and dreams of a man who has known and been loved by many other women. As is usual, most of the principal characters of Act I turn up again in Act II, and it is here, of course, that Bois-d'Enghien discovers that Lucette is to make an appearance that evening. A number of difficult situations develop during which the young husband-to-be attempts to keep his liaison with Lucette from the Baroness and her daughter. He succeeds for a long time, by hiding in a cupboard, dodging in and out of doors, and avoiding the inevitable encounter. He even warns the Baroness that, as the result of an amorous disappointment some years ago, Lucette cannot hear words like "fiancé," "husband-to-be," or "son-in-law" without becoming hysterical. He thus hopes to avoid being introduced to her by the Baroness as one of the above. In a moment of forgetfulness, exacerbated by the violence of General Irrigua, who is pursuing Bouzin about her house, the Baroness mentions that Bois-d'Enghien is Viviane's fiancé, and Lucette faints. The General takes Bois-d'Enghien's apartment key to use as a home remedy in reviving Lucette by pressing it against her spine.

While the contract is being signed in the next room, Bois-d'Enghien, running back and forth between the contract and Lucette, attempts to bring her to an acceptance of the situation. Lucette, however, has other ideas, and while he is being affectionate, she slips a this-tle from a nearby bouquet down his back; she then suggests that he take off his shirt to get it out, while she sees to it that the doors are all locked. In the meantime, she begins to take off her clothes in preparation for her singing appearance. While Bois-d'Enghien is behind a screen, she quietly unlocks the doors, then, wildly embracing him she loudly cries out her love for him. The entire wedding party comes in and is scandalized at what they see. As the act ends, the Baroness breaks off the marriage.

In the third act, we see the hallway and staircase of Bois-d'Enghien's apartment house, on one side, and on the other his dressing room. Bois-d'Enghien returns after spending the night in a hotel, for he had forgotten to reclaim his key after it was used in an attempt to revive Lucette, and his manservant was on his night out. He is scarcely in his apartment and stripped down to his underclothes when Bouzin appears, soon pursued by the General. When they have disappeared, Lucette arrives and Bois-d'Enghien unceremoniously kicks her out. When she threatens suicide he comes out onto the landing to prevent her from doing anything foolish, only to discover that her weapon is a toy gun which shoots out a fan. As Lucette disappears down the stairs, a gust of wind blows shut his door and the young man is caught in the midst of a wedding party coming down from the third floor; they are shocked and disgusted to find a man in his underclothes standing on the landing. Bouzin, who had been hiding from the General inside the apartment, emerges, but shuts the door before Bois-d'Enghien can stop him. Pointing the toy gun at the songwriter, the desperate young man makes Bouzin turn over his pants, and then abandons him to the pursuits of the police who have arrived at the instigation of the shocked wedding party.

Viviane, now madly in love with Bois-d'Enghien, for she sees he is a man of experience sought after by many women, comes to his apartment, accompanied by her proper English chaperon. She has told Miss Betting that they were going to a singing lesson, so, although the Englishwoman does not understand a word of French, the two are forced to sing their dialogue. They are interrupted by the Baroness who objects to Viviane's marriage to Bois-d'Enghien until the sweet young girl points out that since she has compromised herself by coming to his place, he is the only man she can marry now.

Un Fil à la patte shows Feydeau in full stride. The complicated action is set in motion by the cowardice and lies of the hero who cannot bring himself to admit his forthcoming marriage to his mistress. Each ensuing lie or insanely inventive explanation brings on new catastrophes and complications, threatening at almost every turn to reveal Bois-d'Enghien's secret. In true well-made fashion, however, the revelation is held off until the end of Act II, when the marriage is broken and the young man's life is in jeopardy. Act III, which is all denouement, continues to bring new catastrophes. Nightmare-like, Bois-d'Enghien finds himself for the second time in his underwear in a public place.

But nightmare is not reserved for the hero alone. Bouzin must replace him on the landing without his pants, just as earlier he was unwittingly forced to play the role of Lucette's lover, thereby deflecting the General's ire from the true lover. In Kafkaesque fashion, he spends a good part of his time fleeing from a man who for unknown reasons pursues him everywhere.

The comic of situation underscores the role of man as victim, while comical language begins here to take the direction which will lead to those afflicted characters who cannot speak when it rains, or whose cleft palates make them incomprehensible. The General, in his love scene with Lucette, must constantly excuse himself to go to the door and consult with his interpreter in order to find the correct word. Miss Betting, Englishwoman in a French world, is kept by her linguistic ignorance outside the lives of those she serves. Fontanet, orally if not linguistically flawed, makes others suffer more than himself, thanks to his bad breath, but he is already an outsider, separated from the rest of society by odor and above all by unawareness.

Feydeau's first developed picture of the demimonde reveals a world not unlike that of the bourgeoisie: money and marriages are major preoccupations. However, it is the good-hearted *cocotte* who turns out to be most likable and least grasping of all. Indeed, it is she who is financing her ex-husband as well as Bois-d'Enghien (not to mention friends and relatives). Bois-d'Enghien wants to break with her, not because he is in love with Viviane, but because the young girl offers financial security. The entire first act is a tableau of manners, a kind of *Dame aux camélias*, Act I, in a comic key.

The comic techniques in *Un Fil à la patte* are varied and imaginative, revealing character and making an oblique social commentary, as well as suggesting something beyond. They include the classic means of farce: slapstick and the chase. The latter occurs not once, as is usual in Feydeau—at the end of Act II—but at least once in each act.

The details of the chase, and of every other movement in the play, are given with great precision by
Feydeau, now master of his *mise en scène*. The lengthy
descriptions of décor, blocking, and stage tricks show
an author who expects fidelity to his own conception
of his play. At the end of the text is a note advising the
director how best to effect the closing of Bois-d'Enghien's door in Act III, or how to avoid fumbling
through the bouquet of Act I in order to find the calling card.

An immense success at its first presentation, *Un Fil
à la patte* has been revived with great frequency in
France. It entered the repertoire of the Comédie-Française in 1961, and was performed by that troupe in
their New York appearances during the 1965–66 season, long after the New York English première in 1910
under the fanciful title *The Lady from Lobster Square*.

A number of performances in English have utilized
John Mortimer's adaptation, *Cat Among the Pigeons*,
the 1969 London production of which was described
as "a triumph of ingenuity, gaiety, absurdity and horse
laughter." The ingenuity, gaiety and absurdity were
Feydeau's, but the horse laughter belonged only to the
performers, and reminds us that one of the ever-present
pitfalls of *vaudeville* is vulgarity. Despite scantily clad
people bouncing from bedroom to bedroom, Feydeau's
theater never falls to the level of vulgarity. Disciplined
structure and uncompromising acuity of vision give it
an essential elegance. The London production—a saucy
sex comedy and nothing more—failed to find the blend
of style and truth which Feydeau demands.

L'Hôtel du Libre-Echange, 1894
(Hotel Paradiso)

One of Feydeau's most famous plays, and his last in collaboration with Maurice Desvallières, *L'Hôtel du Libre-Echange* forecasts the turbulent second act by its very title. Monsieur Pinglet, like so many husbands in these comedies, has had enough of married life—he only wishes he had seen twenty years ago what his wife would become in twenty years. He would never have married. Ready for a fling, he convinces the wife of his best friend and next-door neighbor, Paillardin, to spend the night with him in order to avenge herself on a husband whose amorous attention to her is suspiciously lukewarm. In the morning's mail comes an envelope of advertisements for the Hôtel du Libre-Echange, and Pinglet quickly makes note of the address.

It so happens that Paillardin, an architect, has been called as an expert to spend the night at a hotel (of course the same one) which has a room supposedly haunted by ghosts. His night out irritates his wife, Marcelle, pushing her into Pinglet's plans, and at the same time freeing her for the evening. Pinglet's wife, in turn, goes off to visit her sick sister; though she locks her husband at home, he escapes by dropping a rope ladder from the living-room window.

Before leaving, however, the Pinglets receive a visit from Mathieu, a friend from the provinces at whose home they had once stayed for several weeks, and whom, in return, they had invited to stay with them in Paris. Taking advantage of their invitation, he now arrives with his four daughters, but the couple tell him that they simply do not have room for so many people, and he decides to find a hotel. When Pinglet whispers to Marcelle their place of assignation for the evening, Mathieu thinks that he is giving him an address, and he makes note of the Hôtel du Libre-Echange.

The maid, Victoire, also intends to use the services of the hotel whose name she has found while cleaning up the ads which Mme Pinglet irritatedly tossed aside. She has been asked to take Paillardin's nephew to his boarding school that evening, but she has other plans for the adolescent, who is more engrossed in his reading of Descarte's philosophical treatise on *The Passions* than he is in the real thing.

At the hotel the characters from the first act gradually pile up, and sometimes there are more than one or two in the same room. Paillardin is ushered into the "haunted" room, but leaves to have a drink before retiring. Mathieu and his daughters are given the same room by a different clerk who does not know that the room is occupied. It is a large dormitory-type room, with two baths, and this allows Mathieu and the four girls to be out of the room proper when Paillardin returns and goes to bed

In the meantime Pinglet and Marcelle arrive and occupy the room across the hall. Having had a big dinner with champagne and followed by a cigar, Pinglet soon becomes ill and goes to the roof to take some air. Marcelle asks for hot water to prepare him some tea, but as she crosses the hall she encounters Mathieu and his daughters who had met her that afternoon at the Pinglets.' They invite themselves in for tea, and Marcelle has scarcely announced that she very rarely sees M. Pinglet when he walks in in his shirt sleeves, now feeling much better.

When Mathieu finally leaves, Marcelle declares she has had enough and is ready to leave, and Pinglet runs off to try to find her hat which he thinks he had with him when he went to the roof. Mathieu and his daughters go into the bathrooms, and Paillardin returns, noting that his toiletries have been disarranged and his cigars stolen. The clerk ascribes this to the ghosts, but Paillardin disdainfully goes to sleep, still skeptical. Mathieu's daughters are preparing for bed when their light goes out, and they begin to dance and sing. Awaking, Paillardin thinks he has been attacked by ghosts. He flees, and finally attempts to enter the room occupied by his wife and her would-be lover, sending Pinglet, who had been holding the door shut, reeling into the fireplace. Marcelle grabs Paillardin's hat and puts it over her entire head as Pinglet, now blackfaced emerges from the fireplace and strikes at Paillardin, who again believes he is being attacked by supernatural beings, and flees from the hotel.

Further complications have, in the meantime, arisen from the arrival of Victoire and Maxime. But they are soon discouraged by the noise and running about, and leave. Finally the police arrive for a vice raid, and all the hotel patrons are taken off to spend the night in jail.

The next morning, Pinglet is back at home, having entered by his rope ladder. His wife, he learns, never arrived at her sister's, and she soon returns to tell him of a horrendous adventure: when the horse pulling her carriage was frightened and ran away, Mme Pinglet (ironically named Angélique) jumped from the vehicle and fainted. She awoke in a thatched hut in some distant village and has just now been brought back to Paris.

Paillardin, unable to waken anyone at home the night before, had spent the night at a friend's. He is unaware of his wife's attempted infidelity. But Pinglet and Marcelle tremble lest their spouses should discover their arrest the night before. They had been allowed to return home when Pinglet, having assumed the name of Paillardin in order to dupe the police into thinking he was with his own wife (a tactic which failed, for Mme Paillardin, with the same thought in mind, had given her name as Mme Pinglet), left a guarantee of 5000 francs.

Pinglet is petrified when his wife receives a summons from the police, reminding her of her arrest the previous night. It was, of course, meant for Marcelle who had assumed the name of Mme Pinglet. Angélique wonders if she has gone mad, and her husband, reading the summons decides to protect himself by accusing her of the guilty act. Paillardin soon receives the summons intended for Pinglet, and Marcelle plays the comedy of the incensed wife. When the police commissioner arrives, he "recognizes" them as the guilty pair he arrested the night before; however, he admits that one had been veiled and that the other had had his face blackened, so he may be making a mistake. Finally he recognizes the guilty pair in Maxime, who inadvertently comes into the room, and the maid who has just put on the new dress given her by Marcelle, for Paillardin's wife had been warned by Pinglet that her husband had said he could not recognize the woman into whose room he ran, but he would recognize the dress anywhere.

Both couples are thus saved, and Maxime too receives a reward: the police commissioner who had recognized in Paillardin's name an important architect, has actually come to excuse himself for the arrests, to ask for advice about a country house in his possession, and to return the 5000-franc guarantee left by Pinglet. Pinglet is out 5000 francs, and he has actually achieved nothing during his night out. He vows never to return to the Hôtel du Libre-Echange. Maxime, however, with his new-found interest in passions outside the textbooks, decides that, if one recieves 5000-franc prizes for going to such places, he will certainly persist.

The preposterous happenings of this *vaudeville*, one following the other at reckless speed, give it a rhythm and verve typical of the best of Feydeau. The structure leading from home to hotel to home is like that of a number of his other plays, and the insane second act, with its proliferation of doors, and all the multiple possibilities they offer played to the full, is a masterpiece of construction and coincidence. The most obvious comic techniques used are those of situation, and those of slapstick—breaking chairs and face blackened with soot.

The highly respected scholar, Henri Clouard, in his

History of French Literature, declares that if there is a masterpiece of *vaudeville*—"a genre in which the pitiless logic of the most preposterously unexpected situations requires that they be prepared and polished with impeccable precision,"—it is certainly *L'Hôtel du Libre Echange* or *La Dame de chez Maxim.*

But *L'Hôtel du Libre-Echange* is more than a clever concatenation of absurdities. It reveals the author's disabused views on marriage, friendship, and the morals of the middle class. Frigid husbands, shrewish wives, ill-assorted spouses, make of marriage—as though time were too often not enough to destroy love and romance —an unbearable state. Illicit love is no better—unless one is young and just learning the pleasures of the flesh, as Maxime does at the hands of the saucy maid. Friends exist to be used, or duped. Materialism is rampant. Whether it is a question of money or of morals, the rule is "an eye for an eye." If the Pinglets have spent two weeks at Mathieu's home, then they owe him a month, since they were two and he is only one. But no more than a month.

This is the first play in which Feydeau introduces a character afflicted with some speech difficulty—he was sometimes to make it realistic, sometimes fantastic. Mathieu stutters when it rains and is reduced to silence by a storm. Such an incomprehensible quirk becomes believable for the characters in the world of farce, but remains enigmatic for us: an embodiment of the absurd. Like Ionesco half a century later, Feydeau treats the unbearable as comical, suggesting through humor a vision which is far from amusing.

After an absence from the French stage since 1931, this work was revived at the Marigny in 1956 with the remarkable Compagnie Grenier-Hussenot. In its English version, *Hotel Paradiso*, Alec Guinness created "a highly intoxicating brew" for the London audiences, while in New York Bert Lahr achieved one of the greatest triumphs of his career. In 1966 a filmed version brought *Hotel Paradiso* to a broader audience.

Le Dindon, 1896
(The Dupe)

Unlike most of Feydeau's plays, this three-act work bears the descriptive word *pièce* after its title, rather than the more precise appellations *comédie* or *vaudeville*. *Pièce* is the most noncommittal word one can use in French for a play, for it implies neither comedy, tragedy, farce, nor melodrama. *Le Dindon* (literally, "the turkey," but its essential meaning is "the dupe," perhaps more imaginatively translated as "holding the bag"), like *Le Bourgeon* and *Le Ruban*, is located somewhat outside the mainstream of Feydeau's production, but not far from that vital current, for it shares many of the comic techniques of the other plays, and certainly partakes in many instances of their violence, energy and movement. But *Le Dindon* possesses a certain seriousness which is lacking in most of the *vaudevilles*—or rather, in this play that seriousness (which is a foundation to all the plays) is more apparent. At moments, indeed, *Le Dindon* reads almost like one of the *pièces à thèse* of Dumas the younger, who was, like Feydeau, a writer of elegant French, a master of the well-made construction, and a man of wit. And yet what is the thesis of *Le Dindon?* If there is one, it is well hidden, as in all this author's works, and we are left to draw our own conclusions about love and conjugal fidelity.

As in many earlier works, we once again find the married couple—but this time not so ill-assorted as in many households—and not one, but two, would-be lovers of the wife. With an unaccustomed seriousness, the author examines various phases of the love relationship both in and out of marriage, but lightens the seriousness with incredible coincidence and preposterous behavior.

Le Dindon begins, *in medias res,* with Lucienne (Mme Vatelin) being pursued into her very living room by a man who has been following her in the streets for the past week. This heated beginning is followed immediately by a *coup de théâtre* as the husband, Vatelin, enters and discovers in the pursuer his friend, Pontagnac. Pontagnac attempts to make him believe that he has simply dropped by for a visit, but Lucienne is pitiless and slowly, comically, exposes his crude behavior. Vatelin, somewhat naively, forgives Pontagnac and explains his wild reputation to Lucienne. When Lucienne discovers that he is married, to boot, she launches into a sermon on conjugal fidelity which might have come straight out of Dumas' *Les Idées de Madame Aubray.* Like all Feydeau wives (and unlike Dumas') she claims recourse to the law of retaliation, and avers that should her own husband ever behave in such a way, she would immediately take a lover.

When the Vatelins express their interest in Pontagnac's wife, he tells them she is bedridden and only goes out pulled in a little cart. When they insist on going to visit her, he explains that on the orders of her physician she lives in southern France.

At this point, an art dealer arrives with a painting Vatelin has purchased, and the husband leaves his wife alone with Pontagnac. In the both witty and serious brief scene that follows, she twits him for his light behavior. They are interrupted by Rédillon, a young man in love with Lucienne. Pontagnac goes off to see his friend's paintings, and we learn that Rédillon has extracted from Lucienne the promise that if ever she should deceive her husband, it would be with him. Pontagnac and Vatelin return from viewing the latter's "unsigned masterpieces," and all four utter a sigh at the thought of poor Madame Pontagnac confined to her little wagon in far off Pau. Immediately she is announced. Suspicious of her husband, and his claim that he goes every evening to the Vatelin's, she has come to look into his activities. Of course he has never been there till this day, and Vatelin very nearly blurts out the truth. He is also astonished to discover that Mme Pontagnac thinks that *he* is bedridden and gets about in a little wagon.

When the two women are left alone, Lucienne quite frankly answers the questions of Mme Pontagnac, who swears to follow her husband's activities closely; should she catch him in the act, she will evoke the *lex talionis*, and turn to Rédillon to be her avenger. Lucienne, moved by Mme Pontagnac's situation, likewise asks Rédillon to be ready for her should she ever need him in this capacity.

A woman arrives, presumably to consult Vatelin in his professional capacity as a lawyer. She is Maggy, an Englishwoman who has come to Paris with her husband. While in London on business sometime ago, Vatelin had had the weakness to make love to Maggy, and now she has come to Paris in pursuit of him. When he refuses to have anything to do with her, insisting that his affair in London was his one momentary lapse from marital fidelity, she threatens suicide. He is forced to agree to meet her that evening at an address she has given him. In the meantime her husband, Soldignac, arrives. He has retrieved from the wastebasket the draft of a love letter arranging a rendezvous for that evening between his wife and her lover. Intending to catch them in the act, he has come to ask Vatelin to draw up the necessary divorce papers.

Vatelin asks Pontagnac, who has returned, to suggest a hotel to which he might take Maggy so that they may avoid discovery by the husband and the police. Vatelin goes off to send a telegram to the Hôtel Ultimus, and Pontagnac joyfully announces to Lucienne that her husband is deceiving her. He warns her that Vatelin will pretend he must leave town on some legal business that very evening, which, in fact, Vatelin does. Lucienne now convinced of his guilt, plans to go to the Hôtel Ultimus to catch him in the act.

At the hotel, the predictable Feydeau chaos will soon break loose as all the major characters of Act I, for one reason or another, appear at the hotel along with a number of new personages. Sooner or later all appear in room 39. Rédillon at first has a rendezvous there with a *cocotte*, Armandine, whom he had flirted with at the theater. Armandine is packing her bags in order to move to a more desirable room, where she has an appointment with another gentleman, a certain Englishman named Soldignac. She is about to send Rédillon away dissatisfied, when he convinces her to stand up the

Englishman and come home with him. Soon an elderly
couple from the provinces are ushered in, Dr. and Mme
Pinchard—a retired army doctor and his stone-deaf
wife. They have come to Paris for their twenty-fifth
wedding anniversary, and they soon leave for the
Opéra to see a ballet.

Pontagnac enters the room, and when he finds the
maid there, pretends he has made a mistake. But during
this time he is able to take the key out of the door
which communicates with the neighboring room,
where he and Lucienne are lying in wait for Vatelin
and Maggy. Pontagnac has brought two electric bells,
which he places under the mattress, one under each
side, so that he and Lucienne in the next room will
know when both parties have gone to bed.

Maggy arrives, soon followed by Vatelin, who is cool
and uninterested. When Maggy threatens double suicide, offering him strychnine-laced tea, he decides to
pretend passion. Maggy goes into the bathroom to undress, there is a knock at the door and Soldignac enters.
In a droll scene he watches his wife's hand stretch
from the bathroom door and deposit her skirt and
blouse on a nearby chair, but when she innocently
walks into the room, Vatelin grasps Soldignac's head
and moves it in the other direction. Finally, along with
Rédillon who has returned looking for a bag left by
Armandine, Vatelin and Soldignac go to play a game
of billiards—this being the only way Vatelin can get the
husband to leave.

Pinchard and his wife now return from the Opéra,
the latter having become ill with her chronic liver ail-
ment. When she lies down the bell under her mattress
is set off, as is the other when Pinchard sits on the bed
to remove his shoes. Lucienne and Pontagnac rush into

the room, knock down the doctor, see their mistake and retreat to the next room before the poor old man can understand what has happened. The maid, the clerk, the bellboy and numerous guests troop into the room complaining of the occupants who are ringing their bell in the middle of the night. Finally the bells are discovered under the mattress, and everyone leaves.

Madame Pinchard, now agitated, is suffering terribly and her husband goes downstairs to the kitchen to prepare her a cataplasm. She goes to sleep, and Vatelin returns and climbs into bed with her, thinking that Maggy has gone to sleep. When Pinchard returns and finds a man in bed with his wife, he raises the roof, bringing Lucienne and Pontagnac from next door in time to see Vatelin grab his clothes (and the chair on which they were hanging), and run from the room. The Pinchards set out after him, followed by Lucienne, who shuts the door in Pontagnac's nose, for it is Rédillon, not Pontagnac, that she intends to make her avenger. When the police arrive with Soldignac they find Pontagnac and drag Maggy out of the bathroom. A second group of police arrive, this time with Mme Pontagnac, and bear witness to her husband's guilty conduct.

The following morning at his apartment, Rédillon is recovering from a night with Armandine when Lucienne arrives, asking him to avenge her. He is so worn-out from the previous night that he can only bleat foolishly, "Lucienne! Lucienne!" Mme Pontagnac arrives, requesting the same service of the exhausted young man, who finally retires to his own room and locks the door.

When Pontagnac comes to make a last effort to convince Lucienne to allow him the privilege of avenging

her, she hides his wife in an adjoining room, and pro-
ceeds to put him in a compromising position by taking
off her own coat and making him take off his coat and
vest and unbutton his suspenders. However, once the
stage is set, she picks up a magazine and refuses to do
anything until someone comes. When voices are heard,
she throws herself into his arms, and the police enter
with Vatelin and recognize her guilt. Madame Pontagnac appears, pointing an accusing finger at her husband. Lucienne, looking Vatelin in the face, arrogantly
admits her "guilt," but it soon becomes apparent that
she is playing a role and is in truth suffering, for she
loves Vatelin. While she and Pontagnac watch the police superintendant write up a report in the back room,
Vatelin breaks down and admits to Rédillon that he is
miserable. When Lucienne walks into the room, Rédillon signals her to be silent, and she overhears Vatelin's
admission of his own fault while in London, his re-
pentance, and his wish to regain the love of a wife
whom he dearly loves. In a touching scene, husband
and wife are reconciled, while Rédillon also weeps sentimental tears. Only Pontagnac is left alone, "holding
the bag."

An immense success at its première, Le Dindon was
revived a number of times, then fell into oblivion until
it was revived in 1951 by the perceptive director of the
Comédie-Française, Pierre-Aimé Touchard. Desperate
over the low receipts at the "second theater" of France
(the former Odéon, in 1951 called the Salle Luxembourg, was the second house belonging to the Comédie-
Française, but used for less classical productions than
the "first theatre," the Salle Richelieu), Touchard had
the brilliant inspiration of reviving Le Dindon after a
twenty-five year absence from the boards. What he

feared most was the selection committee's reaction to the bed onstage in Act II—a prop they might consider unworthy of a state subsidized theater. But selection committee, then audiences and critics were unanimous in their praise. Feydeau's comedy allowed the Salle Luxembourg to survive.

Other Feydeau plays had been performed at the Odéon during the author's lifetime, and as recently as 1941, one of the short plays, *Feu la mère de madame*, had been included in the Comédie-Française repertoire. But *Le Dindon* was the first long play performed in a state theater after World War II. Its success there marked Feydeau's elevation to classical status. During the New York tour of 1961, the Comédie-Française performed *Le Dindon*, and the same year added *Un Fil à la patte* to their Paris repertoire.

Recognized today as one of Feydeau's masterpieces, it is perhaps not surprising that *Le Dindon* had been forgotten for some years. Until recently Feydeau's name was synonymous with frothy *vaudeville*, and this comedy presents, along with the usual mad romp, a serious side with which most theatergoers were no longer familiar. *Le Dindon* is a *vaudeville* (Act II) framed by two acts of comedy of character and manners.

In a relentlessly honest study of love and marriage, Feydeau reveals with the cruelty of one of Anouilh's dark comedies, the fundamental egotism of all men, whether thoughtless playboy (Rédillon), faithless husband (Pontagnac), or cool English businessman (Soldignac). In the pathetic and sometimes touching portrait of the Pinchards, she deaf, he something of a tamed satyr, we see what the future holds in store even for those couples who stick together.

Of the men only Vatelin earns our sympathy, for if

he almost sins, it is unwillingly. But while appealingly
portrayed as a husband, Vatelin is cruelly satirized as
the typical nouveau riche bourgeois—an unimaginative
mediocrity with neither taste nor style.

Lucienne, more imaginative and intelligent than her
husband, exhibits, like almost all Feydeau women, characteristics which were to become exacerbated in the
later plays. Her final scene of forgiveness, with its
clearly intended pathos, is closer to drama than to
vaudeville, and yet Feydeau saves it from sentimentality by his ever-present humor.

Given the more realistic hue of this work, it is not
surprising that the "afflicted" character, deaf Mme
Pinchard, is treated in a more credible way than, say,
Mathieu in *L'Hôtel du Libre-Echange* or Lapige in *La
Main passe*. Her affliction is, indeed, not an uncommon
one. But the suggestion of her nightmare existence is
only one indication in this masterly play of the profoundly pessimistic view of life underlying Feydeau's
baroque frivolities.

Despite serious implications, a general lightness of
tone lifts *Le Dindon* above the dated tedium of its contemporary ideological dramas. Its demonic rhythm, beginning in the second act, leads it into a generic prox-
imity with *L'Hôtel du Libre-Echange* and *La Puce à
l'oreille*. Like those plays, its three acts go from bourgeois home to wildly promiscuous hotel and then back
to the daylight world after a night which can once
more only be evoked by the words: "My God! What
a night!"

La Dame de chez Maxim, 1899
(The Lady from Maxim's)

This most popular of Feydeau's plays during his lifetime, and revived dozens of times since his death—often almost annually—is rarely evoked by Frenchmen without a great sense of nostalgia, and particularly a feeling of affection for the delicious *cocotte*, la Môme Crevette. *La Dame de chez Maxim* is Feydeau's longest play, and one of his most complex in its structure. The situations seem insoluble. Indeed, it is almost impossible to keep in mind all the intricacies that have evolved, and yet with his usual ease and genius, at the end, with one simple maneuver, the author brings all to a satisfactory and happy conclusion.

Doctor Petypon wakes up one morning, after having spent the previous evening at Maxim's with his friend Mongicourt, to find himself on the floor with a terrible hangover, and a strange woman in his bed—the irrepressible and delightfully saucy Môme Crevette, a dancer at the Moulin Rouge. He is shocked first because he is not given to wild nights out, and secondly he is a respectable married man whose wife may enter at any moment. In fact, she does, and carries off Crevette's dress which she finds hanging on a chair and takes to be a dress she had recently ordered. Crevette overhears Mme Petypon reprimand her husband and his friend for their dissolute behavior, and express her deep religious faith—for she has recently seen a vision of Saint Catherine. Crevette then rises on the bed, covered with a sheet, her face bathed in the light of a lamp hidden in the sheets, and speaks with an "angelic voice" to Mme Petypon, who believes she is seeing another heavenly vision. The doctor and Mongicourt pretend not to see, thus convincing the wife that she alone is privileged. The "angel" tells her to go to the Place de la Concorde where a man will speak to her, and from that word will be born a son who will become the savior of France. Mme Petypon, in ecstasy, sets off for the Place de la Concorde, leaving the way free for Crevette to leave— but she has no dress. While she is waiting for Mongicourt to buy her one, Petypon's uncle, General Petypon arrives. He discovers her in Petypon's bed and assumes she is his wife, whom he has never met. Since the General's own wife is dead, he has come to invite Mme Petypon to play the role of hostess in his country chateau at a party given to announce the engagement of his niece. He had written a letter, but since he is passing through Paris he has decided to come by and deliver his invitation personally. Crevette recognizes the name of the groom-to-be; he is a former lover and the knowledge that he is about to marry somewhat rekindles her love for him. She agrees to go to the General's and Petypon is scandalized when he discovers the situation, but helpless to correct it. A dress is brought from the dressmaker's for Mme Petypon, and Crevette takes it and runs off to slip it on. In the meantime Mme Petypon returns, and when the General meets her he is mystified, since he believes he has already met the doctor's wife. He thinks she is Mongicourt's wife, and is astounded by her forward and affectionate behavior with him. Finally he goes off, promising to return soon to pick up Petypon in order to go together to his country place. Crevette, now dressed, leaves promising also to return in time for the departure.

Two men bring in a new chair which the doctor has ordered for his office. It is an "ecstatic chair," a new invention used for therapeutic reasons and which puts the patient to sleep in a state of euphoria, dreaming whatever he most enjoys.

After showing his wife the chair, Petypon tells her he has been called out of town for an urgent operation and sends her off to pack his suitcase. Two men now arrive, followed soon by Corignon, the former lover of Crevette who is to marry the General's niece. He had seen Crevette with Petypon the night before and had insulted him, so now he insists they must fight a duel. When he discovers that Petypon is his fiancée's cousin, the duel is called off. As the doctor is leaving, Mme Petypon opens a letter she has just received—the one mentioned earlier by the General—which invites the two of them to the chateau, asking her to play hostess. She decides that even though her husband cannot go, it is her duty to attend. Petypon rushes off without listening to her, leaving her almost in the arms of a streetsweeper whom Petypon, in a burst of drunken hospitality, had invited to dinner the night before.

The second act, which takes us to the engagement party at the General's chateau, begins as a genre picture of provincial society. The Abbé with his children's chorus in praise of the General, the upper-crust ladies, topped by the Duchess, the Prefect and his wife, soldiers under the General's command—all watching in admiration and sometimes in astonishment the deportment of the General's stunning "niece," the Môme Crevette. The ladies, like Molière's affected young ladies two hundred years earlier, are eager to imitate the latest Parisian dress, language and behavior, and watch every move she makes. Doctor Petypon hovers over her like a mother hen, ready to correct or cover the blunders he fears. A good part of this act is devoted to comedy of manners rather than the usual comedy of situation. Mme Vidauban, who considers herself the most Parisian of the ladies, since she spends a week in Paris each year, carefully imitates the vulgar swinging movement of Crevette's buttocks as she exaggeratedly bows, and each provincial woman tries to outdo the others in simpering and fluttering. In the midst of her high-toned play acting Crevette unwittingly slips in amusing grammatical faults, which Petypon then explains as the latest rage in Paris.

When Crevette is introduced to the young Duke, and learns that he is about to go to Paris, and above all that he is very wealthy, she makes none too subtle advances to him, but without the others seeing. When Petypon remonstrates with her, she performs a movement which we have been shown in the first act, a kind of tic which is meaningless, but finally hilarious. She throws one leg over a chair, and cries out, "Eh! allez donc, c'est pas mon père!" (Aw, go on, it's not my dad!) At first all is consternation, but soon all the provincial ladies are doing it.

The real action gets under way well into the act

when Gabrielle (Mme Petypon) arrives. Fortunately her husband is out of the room. The General is astonished to see her, for he believes she is Mongicourt's wife, and he has not invited her. He is even more surprised when she tells him not to worry, that she will take charge of everything. Gabrielle is stupefied when she is introduced to Mme Vidauban, and the provincial "Parisian" throws a leg over a chair, proclaiming, "Eh! allez donc, c'est pas mon père!" When *all* the ladies perform the ritual, Gabrielle assumes it is a peculiarity of the region and begins to perform it herself, thereby confirming the ladies in their belief that it is the latest Paris fashion.

When Crevette is introduced to Gabrielle, she speaks to her familiarly, referring to a number of fictitious persons as though Gabrielle should recognize them. The poor woman cannot remember ever meeting Crevette, but when she asks various guests who that woman is, they simply laugh in her face, assuming that she is joking, for Crevette is the hostess! When she finally learns that Crevette is Mme Petypon, she assumes she is the General's new wife and embraces her affectionately, calling her, "My aunt!" By now all the guests have decided that Gabrielle is mad.

Crevette is prevailed upon to sing, and she performs one of her suggestive Moulin Rouge numbers, much to Petypon's chagrin. Fortunately, only the soldiers present understand the argot. Soon Crevette, in a moment of abandon, utters a word never heard in the provincial salon, "Merde!" and there is a shocked silence. When she joins in the dancing and at the end turns her fanny to the guests and throws up her skirts in a classical cancan movement, they are again shocked, but still no one questions her identity.

Petypon has succeeded in locking his wife in a room upstairs and now Corignon, the fiancé, arrives. When he meets Crevette, the two decide to elope together. Mme Petypon, who has got out of her room, in which she believes ghosts had locked her, comes to the salon in great fright, looking for a bag she left on the piano. She is searching under the piano when her husband enters and to mask himself turns off the lights. He finally covers her head with a cloth from the piano, and speaking in an "angel's voice," tells her he is her guardian angel and that she must return home. She believes him, and rushes off to pack her bags. Now Mongicourt arrives, bearing the somewhat belated news that Gabrielle is on her way. Petypon asks him to tell the General he has come to take the doctor back to Paris for an urgent operation. Thus Petypon and Crevette can escape this difficult situation.

Crevette and Corignon run off, and when the servant tells the General what has happened, he cries out, "Mme Petypon is a hussy!" Gabrielle, standing nearby, is insulted and slaps him. The General then slaps Mongicourt who enters at this point, for he believes him to be Gabrielle's husband. He challenges him to a duel and then rushes off with Petypon in pursuit of Crevette.

In Act III, the young Duke, who has gotten Petypon's address, comes to call on Crevette, thinking of course that she is Mme Petypon. Gabrielle receives him, and each is irritated by the other. He finally leaves, and sends a letter addressed to Mme Petypon, declaring his love.

Mongicourt arrives, refusing to fight a duel with the General. Petypon claims he has arranged everything by writing a letter to the General, saying that he has forgiven his wife her moment of weakness with Corignon, and is leaving with her for a trip to Italy.

At this point the General arrives with Crevette in tow, and encounters Gabrielle—he finds it strange that Mongicourt's wife is so often at Petypon's house. She asks him to forgive her slap, and he finally does, but says her husband must also apologize. He further advises her to strike the next ghost she sees and that will show her the folly of her faith in the supernatural.

Alone with Petypon, the General convinces him to forgive his "wife," i.e., Crevette, for running off with Corignon, since nothing happened between the two. When Petypon acquiesces, the General sends for the doctor's wife, and of course it is Gabrielle who appears. When the complications seem inexplicable, the General sits for a moment in the ecstatic chair, and Petypon pushes the button, sending him into ecstatic slumber. Gabrielle, not knowing what has happened, rushes up to him, touches him and falls into slumber herself, in a standing position. Petypon instinctively reaches for her, and he also freezes. The servant enters to introduce one of the soldiers from Act II who has come to call on Crevette. The servant joins the petrified group and is soon joined by the soldier. It is only when Mongicourt enters that he realizes what has happened and pushes the button releasing them.

Petypon gets rid of everyone and takes Gabrielle and Mongicourt into the next room, leaving the General alone with Crevette. She makes advances to him, kissing him lingeringly and leads him to believe that Petypon has deserted her for another woman. He seats her in the ecstatic chair, and banging on the table announces that he will bring her husband back to her. His gesture sets the chair in motion, and he leaves her asleep. The young Duke comes in search of her, grabs her hand, and falls into slumber.

The General brings back Petypon to reunite him with his innocent wife, and discovers her being kissed by the sleeping Duke. Petypon releases them, all is forgiven and he is embracing Crevette as his wife walks into the room. When she recognizes Crevette, Gabrielle, who believes her to be the General's wife, kisses her, calling her aunt, thereby corroborating the General in his belief that she is mad.

Gabrielle and Crevette go off, and Petypon, seeing that the General is fond of Crevette admits that she is not his wife, but the General thinks he is joking. The seconds for the duel with Corignon arrive, and without allowing Petypon to participate in the discussion, they decide that he must fight with a pistol. Gabrielle erupts into the room, and will not hear of a fight, clinging to her husband. The General, disgusted, accuses Petypon of having her as mistress, and calls in Crevette to tell her this truth. The General's announcement reveals the truth to Gabrielle, and she is furious, but the General will not believe that she is in reality Petypon's wife. He goes off with Crevette, leaving Petypon asleep, for he had distractedly sat in the ecstatic chair which was left on a moment earlier. Gabrielle slaps him in her anger, but Mongicourt turns off the apparatus and Petypon wakens to his wife's fury. She tells him all is over between them, and Petypon goes off despondently.

At this moment the Duke arrives once more, in search of Crevette. Gabrielle, having read his love letter to "Mme Petypon," finds that he has come at the psychological moment and greets him with open arms, asking him to take her away with him. He flees.

Petypon, in a last desperate effort, disguises himself

in a sheet, as Crevette had in the first act, and speaks with the angel's voice, telling Gabrielle to be kind to her husband. The General enters and Gabrielle, to prove to him that her voices are real, takes one of the swords the General had brought for the duel and attempts to run the ghostly figure through. Of course Petypon flees and is discovered by his wife who, in a classic scene of farce, pursues him about the room, across the bed, and into the next room.

The General tells Mongicourt that Crevette has explained everything, and that Mongicourt must now send on the blow he gave him the evening before by giving it to Petypon, since it was intended for Gabrielle's husband. Petypon and Gabrielle enter, the wife having received a satisfactory explanation from her husband. She explains that Petypon behaved as he did in order to avoid a scandal over the marriage of the General's niece, since he knew that Crevette had been Corignon's mistress. Petypon receives the blow from Mongicourt, and the General goes off affectionately with Crevette, who explains to the others that, after all: "Et allez donc! c'est pas mon père!"

Reviewing the 1965 revival of this play which starred Zizi Jeanmaire, the English critic Kenneth Tynan states, "I agree with Marcel Achard that Feydeau, who died in 1921, was the greatest master of French comedy after Molière, but here he is well below his quicksilver best." French critics—and French audiences—could not disagree more. Scholars and theatermen alike agree that *La Dame de chez Maxim* is one of the summits of Feydeau's work. Obviously it does not possess the serious implications of *Le Dindon* or the virulent satire of *On purge bébé*. But it is the very embodiment of the *vaudeville* form at its zenith, *the* masterpiece of the genre.

La Dame de chez Maxim also contains elements of the so-called higher forms of comedy, particularly the comedy of manners. While most of the characters are types, la Môme Crevette and Gabrielle stand out as individuals, the latter perhaps digging a bit deeper than many of Feydeau's portrayals. Like the stutterers, the deaf, and others afflicted with physical impairments which are used for comic effect, Gabrielle suggests the pathetic side of the human comedy. Unlike them, she is not physically afflicted, although one might make a case for mental affliction, with her simple faith in ghosts and saintly apparitions. But she does share their situation as unwitting victim, particularly in the second act where she fulfills the role of hostess which the General had asked her to play, and all the while the General believes she is mad, and the other guests are laughing behind her back. We almost pity her, but insane events follow one another so rapidly we are not allowed time to sympathize.

At its premiere *La Dame de chez Maxim* was criticized by a few devout members of the audience as sacrilegious, or at least anticlerical. Believers were feeling touchy, as the Church had lost prestige thanks to the support it had given the now clearly guilty military in the Dreyfus affair. The separation of Church and state was only five years away. What particularly shocked these spectators was the scene in Act II in which Crevette sings her vulgar song. Originally Feydeau had the Abbé accompany her at the piano and make remarks which amusingly revealed his total innocence of worldly matters.

At the request of the dowager Duchess of Uzès, Feydeau, with his usual elegance and good taste, consented to delete the offending passage. In a delightfully urbane and profoundly kind letter, he assured her that if the incriminating scene wounded the religious convictions of only a few members of the audience, that was sufficient reason for him to take account of their sensibilities and make the desired changes.

Feydeau had an unfortunate run-in with a certain Professor Moutier, who had actually invented an "ecstatic chair" for medical purposes. Mentioned as its inventor in the play, Moutier objected that the comic use of his invention discredited his name. Feydeau changed the professor's name in the play, but in a 1906 production the true name inadvertently reappeared, provoking a lengthy lawsuit against Feydeau.

The ecstatic chair is the first full-blown gadget in Feydeau's theatre, although earlier plays, like *Un Fil à la patte* and *Le Dindon* had used such objects as bells. Like the revolving bed in *La Puce à l'oreille*, Dr. Petypon's ecstatic chair is responsible for much of the farce in Act III and saves the doctor from several difficult situations.

Examples of pure physical farce abound in *La Dame de chez Maxim*. The ecstatic chair is only one example; but there are more humanly mechanical moments, as when Petypon receives the Duke's kiss originally intended for Crevette, or when the doctor, forgetting that he is holding a chair in his hand, offers to shake hands with the Duke, and after the handshake leaves the Duke holding the chair.

But despite such blatant nonrealistic farcical techniques, the foundation of the play is as surely real as is the ecstatic chair, whose source of origin gave rise to such problems for the author.

As in other works, the *quiproquo* is responsible for the confused events which culminate in the party of Act II, as the General mistakes Crevette for Mme Petypon. The confusion is kept up until almost the very end, and in good well-made play fashion is only ironed out in time for a satisfactory and rapid denouement.

The outrageous behavior of the Môme Crevette at the General's chateau, and the degree to which we accept it, are a tribute to the author's skill. Our acceptance also derives, however, from our recognition of an old tradition of comedy and farce, which goes back at least to the days of Molière: the spoofing of the bourgeois who aspires to nobility, or the provincial who aspires to city-bred status, and thereby reveals his foolishness by imitating unworthy models.

The dexterity with which Feydeau manipulates the several dozen characters in Act II is matched only by his skill in leading them through the maze of complexities which arise throughout the play. As author-director he is concerned that his play be performed realistically. Asides were accepted as part of the theatrical conventions of the day, but when Crevette sings her song for the guests assembled at the General's chateau, Feydeau insisted that she should face the guests and *not* the audience in the theater.

La Dame de chez Maxim introduced to a large Parisian public an actress who was to become the interpreter of all Feydeau's subsequent female leads, Armande Cassive. The dramatist had seen and admired her beauty several years earlier in insignificant operettas, but it was only in late 1898 that he finally was introduced to her and began training her for the part of Crevette. It is said that, quite painfully and insistently, the master taught her syllable by syllable, inflection by inflection, move by move, the role which was to be one of her greatest triumphs. From a mediocre operetta performer, with a voice Feydeau considered unpleasantly nasal, she was to become the unforgettable interpreter of *cocottes*, housewives and bitter shrews.

In 1900, Feydeau and Cassive were in their glory. From all over Europe people came to Paris for two reasons: to visit the Universal Exposition, and to see *La Dame*.

La Main passe, 1904
(Chemin de fer)

La Main passe is one of Feydeau's finest
plays, combining with wit and finesse all the typical
elements of his mature middle style, for which he is
most famous. Like Le Dindon, it is partly comedy of
manners, partly vaudeville.

The marriage of Francine and Chanal is apparently
on the rocks, although this is not clear to the innocent
husband who believes his wife temperamentally incapable of taking a lover. He is not even suspicious when a
colleague, Hubertin, expresses the belief that he has
seen her in the same apartment building where he lives.
Nor does he realize that the famed orator of the Senate,
Coustouillu, who in the presence of Francine is reduced to an almost wordless fool coming and going
with presents to satisfy her least whim, is in love with
his wife. Into this household comes a stranger, Monsieur Massenay, who wishes to rent the apartment
Chanal has for let in the same building. When Chanal
leaves Massenay and Francine alone, they embrace, and

the man explains that he has decided to rent the rooms so that Francine may visit him without going to the trouble of leaving the building. They make plans to meet that evening at Massenay's present apartment, not realizing that their words are being recorded on a phonograph cylinder on which Chanal had been recording a wedding message to send to his sister in America, and which had been accidentally set in movement by Francine's elbow. It is only after the two have left, Francine presumably to go to her mother's for the evening, that Chanal hears the recording and realizes the truth, although he believes the man's voice is that of Coustouillu. As the innocent would-be wooer passes through the room, Chanal shouts at him to go ahead and consummate his adulterous love at 21 Colisée Avenue.

At Massenay's apartment, the adulterous lovers wake up thinking they have just slept a short while and discover to their horror that it is six in the morning. Francine has no excuse to explain such a long absence, and she discovers that Massenay, whom she had thought single, is equally worried about explaining his absence to his wife. While they go off to wash up before dressing, the door opens and Hubertin, Chanal's colleague who lives in the same building, comes in, drunk. His key opens this door and so he believes, although mystified, that he has managed to climb to his own sixth floor apartment by going up only one flight of steps. When he discovers Massenay in the apartment he believes he has been cuckolded and throws the interloper's clothes out the window.

Hubertin passes through the various stages of drunken reaction, from game playing, weeping, through violence and shooting, to sound sleep. At this point

Chanal arrives with the police to catch his wife in the act, and ask for a divorce. Coustouillu, who arrives just as they are leaving, charges into the room, and finding Hubertin in the bed, believes him to be Francine's lover. He strikes him, and the drunk responds with a revolver shot. "What a night!" cries Massenay as he runs off, clasping about his waist Hubertin's immense pants, taken instead of his own which have disappeared from the sidewalk below.

At Massenay's home his wife, sweet and unsuspecting Sophie, is waiting anxiously for her missing husband, fearing him perhaps dead. Belgence, a family friend and her hopeful admirer, has brought a police commissioner to help find Massenay, but he is more interested in advancing himself by means of an important case than he is in the welfare of Massenay. A stone-mason arrives, Lapige, who has found Massenay's clothes on the sidewalk. He is afflicted with the congenital habit of barking whenever he becomes excited, so it is some time before he can explain how he came by the clothes. His explanation is enough to throw a stick in the wheels of Massenay's absurd invention when he finally walks in. He claims that he was carried off by a train which left without warning while he was saying farewell to some friends. During his return trip from Amiens he awoke to find himself dressed in these large pants, his own clothes gone, and a strong smell of chloroform in the compartment. His innocent wife believes his story, even when he is pursued in nightmarish fashion by the drunk Hubertin, who has found his address and come, dressed only in overcoat and top hat, to claim his pants. After pistol shots and a good deal of tugging, Massenay has finally got Hubertin into an adjoining room, when Chanal arrives, having calmed down and reached the decision that, since Massenay and Francine love each other, they must divorce and remarry. "Now it's your hand," he tells the weary lover, thus giving the play its title. A moment later Francine's trunks are brought over and Massenay is faced with the unpleasant duty of explaining things to his wife. He is saved the trouble when the policeman Planteloup returns triumphantly with the news that he now knows the train story was a subterfuge, for Massenay was caught *in flagrante delicto* that very night with Mme Chanal. Sophie slaps her husband on one cheek and storms out. Coustouillu, having found the true culprit, strikes him on the other.

The final act takes place some months later. Massenay and Francine are now married, and the wife's life made unbearable by her husband's constant suspicions and jealousy. Chanal, who returns for a visit, is delighted to hear they are getting on so badly, for he has begun to feel he might like to be back with Francine again. Massenay's presence and constant fussing only irritate Francine, who tells him that he is pushing her too far and that she will take a lover simply to justify his suspicions. Coustouillu arrives at this opportune moment and she leads him off, as Belgence is announced. Belgence now hopes to marry Sophie, and has come at her insistence, to get Massenay's permission. When he hears that she is waiting below, apparently still fond of her former husband, he insists that she come upstairs. A reconciliation is effected, much to the horror of Belgence, for Massenay decides to divorce Francine and remarry Sophie. When Coustouillu, no longer stammering or stumbling over furniture, reappears with Francine, and requests the rental of the adjacent apartment which Massenay had asked for in

Act I, the husband realizes what is about to take place, and happily gives it to him, for he is ready now to pass his hand on to another.

The experienced man of the theater that Feydeau had become by the time he wrote this masterly work, is revealed at every turn. The descriptions of the settings and actions are given in great detail by the man who was director as well as author of his play. There are appended notes describing nuances of role interpretation, and setting forth with precision the meaning of left and right as given in the stage directions. As always these directions are of such complexity and importance that they must be followed quite literally if the play is to be fully effective and the actors and props are to come out at the correct place at the proper moment.

The role of movement and pantomime is large in this play, as is the place given to characters with those comical afflictions which had found favor in earlier plays. Coustouillu is the first of these, a man rendered so painfully timid by his undeclared love for Francine that he is literally incapable of speaking an entire sentence in her presence, and is inclined to run into chairs upon entering or leaving a room.

Lapige represents a case beyond the limits of credibility, with his excited barking in moments of stress. The daring characterization prefigures surrealism by ten or fifteen years, and the Absurd theater by half a century.

Hubertin, the drunk, belongs to the same kind of nightmare world, even though his affliction, unlike those of Coustouillu and Lapige, is willingly assumed. Once drunk (and he is drunk in all but his first brief appearance), he is the victim of forces beyond himself—his eyes open with childish wonder at the miracles accomplished in this inebriate state. As Feydeau makes clear, he is not brutishly drunk, but lucidly so, and he possesses an elephantine charm as he bulldozes his way through Massenay's bachelor rooms and later into his home. Massenay, pursued into his very living room by this gun-toting apparition in long underwear, is also the victim of a nightmare from which he would like to waken, but which he has quite clearly brought upon himself.

Gross as these comic devices may strike us when described, Feydeau is too expert to let them get out of hand, and in this play he handles them with a lightness and deftness that reflect the taste and polish of long years of apprenticeship. Lapige, with one bark too many, might have become tedious and annoying—but he is onstage so briefly that we are only allowed the time to be astonished and amused by his improbable affliction. Hubertin is presented with such humor and taste, such a child-like charm, that he is never offensive, even when disrobing before Sophie's amazed eyes. And Coustouillu is painted with such compassion that we suffer with him even as we laugh.

The characters of *La Main passe* belong to the familiar world of bourgeois marriage. Like the other inhabitants of that world they are selfish, blind and self-satisfied. Francine, waking up with Massenay at 6 A.M., tells her lover to stop talking about *his* unfortunate situation—after all, her own situation is even more unfortunate. Bickering like a long-married couple, they form a picture of illicit love as unattractive as marriage itself. Indeed, in *La Main passe* Feydeau suggests that, married or not, love is rarely a bed of roses.

Francine, one of the few faithless wives in Feydeau's world, is already Massenay's mistress when the action of the play begins. "If only husbands would let their wives have one or two lovers, so they could compare," she complains to Chanal after their divorce, "there would be a lot more faithful wives in the world." They would presumably discover that on close contact lovers are no more desirable than husbands.

Without moral condemnation, Feydeau presents his amused and disillusioned picture of marriage. It is a picture which is surprisingly modern, with its easy rhythm of divorce and marriage in the game of musical beds. No wonder *La Main passe*, after an absence of almost thirty years (from 1904 to 1933) has become one of Feydeau's most often revived plays.

In the United States, under the title *Chemin de fer* (a strange "translation," since the English title is even more mysterious to the average theatergoer than is the French), it has had successful runs in Los Angeles, Washington, and New York. A production in Cleveland during the summer of 1974 advertised, "Feydeau's rediscovered masterpiece." But it is a masterpiece that was rediscovered three or four decades ago. The 1941 production in Paris, for which Jean Cocteau designed the costumes, was, according to the critics, as fresh as at its first performance.

Le Bourgeon, 1906
(*The Sprout*)

Le Bourgeon enjoys a certain critical esteem and has even been revived a number of times. Although it is not in the usual dazzling farcical style of Feydeau, it contains reminders of his brilliant comic genius. Its rank, however, is probably due to its more serious tone. The three-act work is classed as a "comédie," but that word is here used in its most general meaning in French —simply a play—for it is only intermittently comic. It approximates in many ways the serious plays of the nineteenth century, like those of Dumas the younger or François de Curel. For us, its chief value lies precisely in this fact: it is Feydeau's only "serious" play, and as such allows us to examine his techniques without being blinded by the hilarious comic devices. It reminds us that he belongs squarely in the nineteenth-century tradition of the well-made play, but his genius allowed him to carry that form to an awesome perfection in its comic form. *Le Bourgeon,* while a fine play, is no finer than a number of other well-written plays of its genre.

Maurice, a young nobleman born into an extremely devout, not to say bigoted, family, intends to become a priest. However his health seems to suffer from his efforts to deny the call of the flesh. A doctor suggests to the horrified mother, the Countess, that he had best be pushed toward some woman who would see to it that the saps of this budding tree (*bourgeon*) serve their natural function. A woman has only recently attempted to rent the carriage house on the Countess's estate, but was refused when it was discovered that she was an actress. Opportunely, this same woman, Etiennette, almost drowns in the nearby ocean, and is saved by Maurice. Her savior wakens warm feelings in her breast, but when she sees him in his seminary uniform, she represses those feelings.

Maurice, now in Paris to begin his military service, comes regularly to visit Etiennette, who has undergone a kind of conversion, identifying herself with Mary Magdalene, as she adores her own savior with a kind of holy awe—perhaps a disguise for a love she feels impossible. In a hilarious scene, Maurice visits with the *cocotte*, unaware of her real profession, and meets her *cocotte* friends whom he takes for ladies of good society. Weaving from *quiproquo* to *quiproquo* in familiar fashion, they convince him that they are indeed very Christian ladies.

The Countess, having decided her son's health is more important than his chastity, comes to Etiennette and begs her to take Maurice as a lover in order to save his health. The *cocotte* is revulsed at the idea, for she idealizes the young man, and she convinces the Countess that such a move would be wrong. In the meantime, the Countess's sister, the comically bigoted old maidish Eugénie, discovers her husband, whom she had considered a model of Christian virtue, in this house cavorting with a *cocotte* friend of Etiennette's.

As the act ends, Etiennette, intending to say farewell to Maurice before he leaves for his army service, suddenly comes to the realization that her love for him is far from chaste. With the sure hand of the professional in love, she leads him to the precipice, and as the curtain closes, they fall into each other's arms.

In the final act, Maurice brings Etiennette back to his mother's country estate to announce his plans to marry. The entire family is shocked, and Maurice's young cousin, Huguette, disappointed, for she had thought one day she might marry the young man. Etiennette realizes the impossibility of their dream, and, perhaps a bit too easily, convinces Maurice that he must follow his mother's wishes. Realizing that Huguette loves her cousin, the "whore with a heart of gold" insists that Maurice accept the girl as his wife—not now, but in a year or so. On this note the play ends, with all restored to order in the world of the good, decent, bourgeois aristocracy.

It is difficult to see this play as highly original, for it conforms in almost every way to the patterns of the well-made play, and indeed of the thesis play which brought Scribe's formulas a degree of seriousness and ideological content. The butt of Feydeau's criticism and satire is the religious bigotry and class consciousness of the wealthy aristocrats (and one might extend this to the bourgeoisie) who are more than outspoken— they are cruel and inhuman—in their treatment of those below them in station. Unlike Dumas, Feydeau is too modern and sophisticated to use a mouthpiece, although he comes perilously close to it in the person of the Countess's brother who, skeptical and urbane, is perfectly willing to see Maurice seduced, but finally balks at the idea of marrying beneath one's class. Feydeau's dislike of bigotry, hypocrisy and self-righteousness is sufficiently clear, particularly when he singles out certain characters (and characteristics) for pointed satire, as in the case of Eugénie.

The structural similarity to the well-made play is not overly obvious, but there are a number of points of comparison. The *scene à faire* is carefully prepared from the start, so that at Act II's curtain, one is not surprised. We even heave a sigh of relief when Maurice falls upon the sofa with the seductress. The use of coincidence and chance, while not exaggerated as in the farcical pieces, does allow the introduction of conventional structural elements: the rising pitch of excitement as the first act curtain nears, followed by a dramatic rebound of the action as the Countess begs the "lost woman" to stay. As the pendulum set in motion in Act I picks up momentum in the following act, we begin to wonder whether Maurice will or will not fall, and as the act ends, we are deeply satisfied by the inevitability (and the justice) of what we witness. The third act is there, however, to return virtue to the world, and in a sense to revolt us by the triumph of the Pharisees.

One is tempted at every turn to see in *Le Bourgeon* a reworking of Dumas' famous *Les Idées de Madame Aubray*. Even the characters conform to the pre-established types: the good-hearted fallen woman who is redeemed by love (Etiennette), the naive young man who loves her (Maurice), the all too Christian mother who finds it difficult to carry her principles to their logical conclusion when the case is too personal (the Countess), the mocking libertine who forms part of the in-group (the Countess's brother), and the sweet young innocent who dares not declare her love but is overwhelmed with sorrow when the wicked woman seduces the young man she secretly loves (Huguette).

There is more psychological complexity in these characters than we find in a number of Feydeau's lighter works, but they are no richer than the creatures in *La Main passe* or *Le Dindon*. There is a danger of being blinded by the comedy to more serious qualities of Feydeau's greater farces, as there is a danger of thinking a more serious play is of greater depth simply because it is not so obviously amusing. Paul Valéry reminded us that "Fools believe that jesting means not being serious." We need not denigrate *Le Bourgeon*, which is a good piece of theatre, but at least three or four of Feydeau's most preposterous *vaudevilles* are deeper and more serious than this apparently serious play.

La Puce à l'oreille, 1907
(*A Flea in Her Ear*)

Perhaps the most popular of Feydeau's plays today, and surely the most often performed in English, *La Puce à l'oreille* uses the ancient theatrical trick of twin characters who are not related. The roles of Victor-Emmanuel Chandebise and Poche are played by the same actor, the author having supplied plentiful notes describing the quick change techniques which allow the performer to disappear at one side of the stage and reappear almost immediately at the other in a completely different costume. The humor of the double identity is increased by the worlds which separate the two characters—one a rich bourgeois and the other a hotel boy—and the cases of mistaken identity, dear to *vaudeville* and farce, which arise.

Chandebise admits to his friend, Dr. Finache, that he has recently been unable to consummate the love act with his wife. His wife, Raymonde, almost simultaneously, confesses her suspicions to her childhood friend, Lucienne. Since Chandebise has ceased to "perform," his wife believes he is betraying her. In order to catch him red-handed, she decides to write an anonymous letter to him, requesting a rendezvous. To disguise the handwriting, she asks Lucienne to write the letter.

When Victor-Emmanuel receives the note, he is tickled, but then realizes it must be a mistake and turns it over to his friend, Tournel, a dashing young man who, unknown to Chandebise, is attempting to seduce Raymonde. Since the anonymous admirer claims she saw him at the theater on an evening when he was accompanied by his friend, Chandebise assumes she mistook Tournel for him.

Claiming that she is going off for dinner and the night at her mother's, Raymonde leaves for the assignation she has made to entrap her husband. Chandebise is about to set off for a banquet he mistakenly believes to be scheduled for this evening, when Lucienne's husband, a flamboyant and excitable Latin American, Homenides, arrives. When Chandebise fatuously shows him the letter from his "secret admirer," the irate Latin recognizes the handwriting as his wife's, and he threatens to kill almost everyone in sight. Chandebise defends himself by saying it is Tournel who is going to the assignation, and Homenides sets off to catch the guilty pair in the act.

Chandebise's nephew, Camille, who works for his uncle, and is looked upon as a model of good behavior, is, in fact, quite the playboy and is apparently carrying on with Antoinette, the maid, who is married to the valet Etienne. He attempts to warn Tournel, but Camille is one of those afflicted characters in Feydeau: he has a cleft palate and can scarcely enunciate his words. Since Camille has misplaced the silver palate Dr.

Finache has made for him, Tournel can understand nothing he says, and he sets off for the rendezvous unaware of the danger threatening him.

At the definitely shady Hôtel du Minet Galant, the audience is allowed to see the front desk, one bedchamber, the stairs and a number of doors and corridors—all of which will serve in the mad scramble about to take place. The hotel proprietor, Ferraillon, is a former soldier, and something of a sadist. His wife, a former *cocotte*, Olympe, delights in the beatings he gives her, as does the half-dazed hotel boy, Poche, once his subaltern in the army. Poche, given to drink, and never too bright, enjoys the kicks in the rear which are his usual diet at the hands of Ferraillon.

An energetic Englishman occupies one room, and regularly comes out asking if anyone has come for him yet. The bedroom visible to the audience is equipped with one of those gadgets which play an important role in Feydeau's later plays. The bed is placed upon a turntable; a button at one side, when pushed, causes the entire bed and section of the wall to turn, bringing into the room the bed in the adjacent room and permitting the illicit couple in the visible bed to disappear into the next chamber. The neighboring bed brings into view an old uncle of Ferraillon who is paid to lie in bed reading and complaining of his pains. Thus are suspicious spouses put off the track, should they trace a wife or husband to this *galant* hotel.

Two major sources of confused identity are supplied by the resemblance of Poche to Chandebise, and by the arrival of two telegrams, each signed simply "Chandebise." One is from Raymonde and the other from Camille, who has an appointment with Antoinette. In her telegram, Raymonde has said to show into the room reserved in that name anyone who asks for Chandebise's room.

Raymonde arrives, and while she is in the washroom adjacent to her chamber, Tournel arrives. He sits on the bed, hidden by the curtains, so that when Raymonde emerges and gives a hearty slap on the face to the man she believes to be her husband, he is quite taken aback. Raymonde, too, is surprised. Unlike most women in Feydeau's world, she has insisted that though her husband is faithless, she *cannot* betray him, because she is too upset. Tournel attempts to convince her that, since Chandebise sent him instead, the husband is faithful, therefore the wife *can* be unfaithful. Raymonde, with the Feydeau woman's usual naive understanding of the role of mistress, is willing to go only so far, and leaves poor Tournel still hungry. When the eager lover goes to lock the door, the frightened woman tries to ring the bell to summon help. Instead, she pushes the button which switches the bed with that of the neighboring room. In a nightmarishly hilarious scene, Tournel turns back from the door and leaps onto the bed, embracing Ferraillon's old uncle instead of Raymonde. Raymonde, fleeing, mystified, from the next room, sees Poche in the hall and believes it is her husband. She is terrified lest he find her with Tournel. When they press the button to return old uncle Baptistin to his former room, the original bed revolves with Poche sitting in it, guzzling the vermouth he has brought up for a guest. Raymonde and Tournel take his indifference for the coldness of a wounded husband, and beg his forgiveness, insisting that he kiss each of them.

Now Camille arrives with the maid, Antoinette, but they encounter Poche and flee, thinking him Chandebise. Antoinette seeks refuge in the Englishman's room, while Camille rushes into the room behind that of Raymonde and Tournel. When they push the button to return Baptistin to his own room (Poche had earlier revolved the bed in an attempt to have Baptistin vouch for his identity), the bed brings in Camille who had sought refuge in the next room. All flee in various directions, Camille into the Englishman's room where he finds Antoinette surrendering to the occupant; he is unceremoniously kicked out and in the ensuing struggle loses his silver palate. Raymonde and Tournel, attempting to leave the hotel are stopped by the arrival of the valet, Etienne, who has come to warn Lucienne of the imminent arrival of Homenides. Instead, he discovers his own wife with the Englishman.

Lucienne arrives—having agreed to help Raymonde confront Chandebise—and is soon followed by Chandebise who has discovered his banquet is the following evening. He has come to warn Lucienne also. They are interrupted by the arrival of Homenides, and all scatter. Ferraillon, the hotelkeeper, mistakes Chandebise for Poche and gives him the usual treatment of kicks in the rear, finally putting him into Poche's livery. Poche, not finding his livery, puts on the clothes discarded by Chandebise. Raymonde encounters her husband, but now believes him to be Poche, until he cries out at her. She flees. Lucienne, finding Poche, believes him to be Chandebise and asks for his protection. He takes her into Baptistin's room. Homenides arrives in a fury, rushes into the Chandebise room, and finding it empty, shoots at the button by the bed, which resembles a target. The bed turns, revealing Poche (whom he takes for Chandebise) and his wife, Lucienne. He is stopped in his pursuit by the other people at the hotel.

Act III takes place back at Chandebise's home. Antoinette, by means of a gratuity, has arranged for the concierge to tell her husband that she had not been out all evening. Poche arrives to return Chandebise's clothing he had put on, and is astounded to find all the people from the hotel in this one house. They in turn believe him to be Chandebise, and think he has gone mad since he will not admit his identity.

When Chandebise returns, Camille thinks he is going mad himself, for he has just seen the same man in bed in his bedroom. Ferraillon arrives and again kicks and strikes Chandebise, believing him to be Poche. Homenides arrives and pursues Poche, who finally jumps out an open window. Homenides discovers the first version of his wife's "love letter" to Chandebise and begins to wonder about the veracity of his suspicions. Raymonde explains the situation to him and the passionate Latin forgives his wife, and explains the truth to Chandebise. The angered husband now understands why he found his wife with Tournel at the hotel and he also is ready to forgive.

La Puce à l'oreille is a well-made play with a vengeance. Instead of the usual secret, shared with the audience, but unknown to one or several characters, there are a number of secrets. The true meaning of Chandebise's lack of passion is hidden from his wife until nearly the end of the play; the meaning behind the anonymous letter of admiration, and the identity of its true writer, are likewise kept secret until almost the final scene. The same is true of the identity confusion arising from Chandebise's resemblance to Poche. In his usual fashion, Feydeau piles complication on complication, and encounters which should lead to clarification, only help to confuse.

The use of the letter is a well-worn device from melodrama and the *vaudeville* of Scribe. Without a letter to start events rolling, to make unexpected revelations (most often false), or to clear up mysteries, the well-made play would be unthinkable—indeed, it is difficult to imagine the nineteenth-century theater bereft of letters which, from Guilbert de Pixerécourt—"the father of melodrama"—through Romantic drama, the comedy of manners, and right up to Naturalism, play an important role.

The flea which is placed in Raymonde's ear, and which sets off succeeding events, is the result of her husband's sexual impotence. Although Feydeau was not an admirer of the Naturalist school, it is difficult to overlook the themes this play shares with writers like Zola. Less heavy-handed, and certainly with no axe to grind, Feydeau presents a tableau of alcoholism, prostitution, sexual perversions or inadequacies, and a general attitude toward life which reflects, on the bourgeois level, the same preoccupations that Naturalism reveals among the workers.

Realism of concept, if not of tone, is apparent in the scene at the hotel where Tournel finally believes he is about to possess the woman he covets. Far from the idealism imagined by the naive young wife, who thinks she can be a mistress without going to bed, the ardent Tournel is precise enough in his amorous aims, rejecting scornfully her offer of only head and heart. The anatomical center of *La Puce à l'oreille* is situated well below the heart.

But all the anatomy of this comedy is not reserved for love. Camille, like many other Feydeau characters, is afflicted with a physical impairment which makes communication difficult. Like them, he is a victim upon whom some monstrous joke has been perpetrated. During the course of the play, however, the breathless spectator has no time to reflect on the threatening parallels between Camille and himself.

Afflicted or not, many of Feydeau's characters are victims of a gigantic machine in which they are caught, and which, in *La Puce à l'oreille* at any rate, brings them to the edge of insanity as they try to get their bearings in the mad world of the Hôtel du Minet Galant. The seventh scene of Act II is pure nightmare, as the characters are plunged into the absolutely incomprehensible and we the audience attacked through our nerves by the absurdity and extremity of the situations in the most violently physical of *vaudevilles*.

Tournel, turning back from locking the door so that he can better violate Raymonde, leaps onto the bed, which in the meantime has revolved, and finds himself embracing Baptistin. For him, as for Raymonde on the other side of the wall, there can be no explanation but madness.

Less convulsive is the nightmare adventure of Chandebise, victim of his identity with Poche. Mistreated by Ferraillon, with no hope of convincing him of his mistake, Chandebise is confronted by the inscrutable mystery of suffering imposed for reasons impenetrable.

La Puce à l'oreille was a triumph when first performed in 1907. Unfortunately the élan of its run was interrupted by sickness in the cast, and when the play resumed performances, its impetus had been broken. It lasted less than two months, and was not revived until 1944. It made up for lost time with frequent revivals thereafter, entering finally into the repertory of the Comédie-Française.

Performances at the Old Vic, with Albert Finney, were very successful in 1965, and were revived for the next few years, including a stint by Laurence Olivier in the role of the butler, Etienne. A film was made in 1968.

Across the Atlantic, this most diabolically contrived of all *vaudevilles* has been performed more than any other Feydeau play, being a favorite with colleges and universities, summer stock companies, and regional theaters. Its productions literally cover the continent, with performances from Seattle to Sarasota, Florida, from San Francisco to Halifax, Nova Scotia, with stops at Dallas and Chicago. The first professional New York production on record took place when the American Conservatory Theatre took their balletic production, directed by Gower Champion, for guest performances on Broadway.

Occupe-toi d'Amélie, 1908
(*Keep an Eye on Amélie*)

By common consent one of Feydeau's masterpieces, this three-act *vaudeville* holds the prime place in the *Théâtre complet* of Feydeau: the first play in the first volume.

Following his usual practice, Feydeau apparently put the play into rehearsal after finishing only the second act. The nervous producer saw the opening date approaching, yet no final act was forthcoming. According to one story, two of the author's actor friends accompanied the lazy dramatist home from Maxim's one night, and Feydeau improvised the famous marriage scene in the early hours of the morning, while his friends wrote it down.

After casting his keen glance at the world of bourgeois marriage in *La Main passe* (1904) and *La Puce à l'oreille* (1907), with a serious nod to the demimonde in the drama *Le Bourgeon* (1906), Feydeau once again plunges us into the gay and carefree world of the *cocotte*. Amélie, like her spiritual sister, Lucette Gautier in *Un Fil à la patte*, is an entertainer, and like Lucette she is generous enough to support her entire family. One of the surprising moments in Act I comes when she slaps her valet whom she has found tippling from a bottle of chartreuse. The young man strikes her right back, and a fight ensues. Only then do we discover that Adonis is her younger brother whom she has taken into her employ. Her father, a former traffic policeman, is another hanger-on. Classically automatic, he continues to exercise his profession even in Amélie's salon, enriching his frequent malapropisms with such locutions as "Move on!" or with official jargon peppered with mistakes.

The first act begins with a tableau of manners, as we witness a gathering in Amélie's salon. Etienne, her lover, is about to go off to do his twenty-eight days of military service. In the midst of the gathering a distraught woman, Countess Irène, arrives. Although married, she is in love with a young man, Marcel, and among his papers has found the first draft of a letter which Marcel had written to his godfather, announcing his marriage to Mlle Amélie d'Avranches. Amélie and Etienne find the idea hilarious and assure Irène that there is not a word of truth to it. Marcel arrives, and explains that, in order to receive an inheritance managed by his godfather, he must be married. Since he cannot marry Irène, he has written his uncle Van Putzeboum (who lives in Holland) that he is marrying Amélie, and he has sent a photograph. Not content with the letter, the uncle has just arrived in Paris in order to meet the girl in person, and he is due to arrive at any moment.

In the meantime, General Koschnadieff makes an appearance. He comes on behalf of the Prince of Pales-

tria who, on a former visit to Paris had seen Amélie
at the Opéra and fallen in love with her. Now back in
Paris, he wishes a rendezvous. Amélie hesitates, since she
already has a lover, but her father, once he understands
the suitor is royalty, urges her to accept.

This conversation is interrupted by Van Putzeboum's arrival. He is pleased to find Marcel in a "decent
family setting," and tickled to kiss Amélie's "virginal
cheek." The play will henceforth deal with Amélie's
and Marcel's efforts to hide the truth from Putzeboum,
who is just dense enough not to understand the situation, although on all sides he is shown convincing proof
of Amélie's true profession.

While the uncle is off making a phone call, Etienne
asks his old friend Marcel to take care of Amélie while
he is off doing his service. Then before leaving, he takes
Amélie into the bedroom for a farewell. At this point
the Prince of Palestria arrives to see Amélie. Her father
puts on a record of the *Marseillaise*, lights a candle and
greets the Prince by kissing his hand. But he cannot get
Amélie's door open, and as the curtain falls, voices from
inside shout, "You can't come in!"

The second act takes place in Marcel's bachelor apart-
ments, where the young man, after a night of carousing,
wakes up to find himself in bed with Amélie. Since he
had been asked to look after her, he is quite disturbed,
particularly since both of them were so drunk the night
before they are not certain just what has taken place
between them.

While Marcel opens his mail—and discovers that his
uncle Van Putzeboum is back in town and wants to
dine with them that evening—Amélie writes a note to
her father asking him to bring her a simple afternoon
frock so that she can dress and leave. To free herself

for the evening, she also writes a note to the Prince of Palestria breaking their appointment. She sends the two letters with the maid to be delivered, and just has time to hide under the bed before Marcel's mistress, Irène, comes into the room. Irène has freed herself for the entire day and insists that Marcel come to bed, beneath which Amélie makes droll comments, wondering if she is to hear a full performance taking place over her head. She manages to pull the bedspread from the foot of the bed and ties it with some string that had earlier fallen to the floor. Covered by the spread, she escapes to the bathroom—and sends the bedspread swishing back to its original place by means of the string which she had carefully turned around one leg of the bed. During this Irène has been telling Marcel of a frightening nightmare, and the ghostly movement of the bedspread is enough to terrify her. When she finally tries to enter the bathroom, Amélie comes rushing out covered with a bathrobe and a mask picked up in the carousing the night before. Irène flees, as does the maid, and Marcel discovers the apparition's identity just in time to dive into bed in an effort to hide from Van Putzeboum. The old uncle bustles into the room and is astounded to find Amélie in bed with her "fiancé," but the *cocotte* greets him in such a relaxed and sophisticated manner that Van Putzeboum responds in an equally worldly and understanding way. He has arranged his business affairs, he tells them, so that he can attend their wedding.

Amélie's father arrives, and after they get rid of Van Putzeboum, he announces the imminent return of Etienne, his twenty-eight days having been shortened to fifteen because of an outbreak of mumps in the regiment. He is interrupted by the arrival of the Prince who has received the letter intended for Amélie's father. He announces he will soon be followed by Koschnadieff bringing a selection of afternoon frocks. While Amélie dresses, a scene of misunderstanding takes place between the Prince and Marcel, whom the noble believes to be the landlord of the building. Van Putzeboum returns while the Prince is attempting to take Amélie on his knees, and everyone dashes into the adjoining room to escape Van Putzeboum.

While the uncle is wondering where everyone could have gone, Etienne arrives. Van Putzeboum, not realizing Etienne's relation to Amélie, confides to him that Marcel and Amélie have slept together. Etienne, furious, vows to avenge himself.

When they get rid of Van Putzeboum again, Marcel explains the difficulties engendered by Van Putzeboum's presence, and Etienne offers to solve everything by arranging a simulated wedding ceremony at the city hall. A friend of his will impersonate the mayor (who, in France, performs the important civil ceremony), and after the ceremony Marcel will receive the money and be free of Van Putzeboum. Amélie and Marcel rejoice in the clever plan, while Etienne gloats over the revenge he will thus be able to take.

The first scene of Act III, in the city hall, is one of Feydeau's skillfully managed crowd scenes, and here based upon an enormous *quiproquo*. Marcel and Amélie, along with their friends, believe that the wedding ceremony is only a pretense, performed by Etienne's friend who sports prominently on his nose a "false" wart. The mayor, however, rightly believes this to be a true wedding ceremony, and is perplexed and then outraged by the lighthearted joking attitudes of the members of the wedding party. The bride and groom find the mayor's seriousness hilarious, believing that he is acting his role to the hilt. They are titillated also by the wart on his nose, which they believe to be a very successful imitation. Many of the guests approach the mayor in order to get a better view and to comment on his wart's realism.

When the ceremony is over, Amélie rushes home for an appointment with the Prince, and Marcel discovers to his horror that the mayor is, in fact, the mayor, and that he and Amélie are in truth man and wife.

At Amélie's apartment, the Prince is waiting for her in his underclothes. When Amélie has removed her outer garments, the Prince begins to embrace her, only to be interrupted by Marcel who comes bearing the catastrophic news. Unlike Marcel, however, Amélie is thrilled, and jumps into his arms, while the Prince, still in underclothes, congratulates the new husband.

In order to obtain a divorce, Marcel now decides he must catch Amélie in adultery. He tosses the Prince's clothes out the window, and goes across the street to the police station to fetch official witnesses to his wife's infidelity. The officers, however, when they discover the Prince's rank, refuse even to recognize that anything unusual has taken place.

Etienne arrives at this juncture, and Marcel in desperation pulls a gun from his pocket and demands his friend's pants. He passes them to the Prince who dons them and leaves. When the police officer returns with the Prince's clothes which had been tossed out the window, he finds Etienne pantless in the room, and agrees to charge him and Amélie with adulterous behavior.

Van Putzeboum arrives and gives a check for his fortune to Marcel before he discovers that the young man is about to divorce Amélie. But, after all, he agrees, the conditions *have* been met, and were even met before the wedding! As the others leave, they push Amélie onto the knees of Etienne, who has collapsed on a canape, and advise him to "Take care of Amélie."

Gayer than Feydeau's other major works since *La Dame de chez Maxim*, perhaps because there is no bourgeois marriage in view, *Occupe-toi d'Amélie* is the bedroom farce par excellence containing not one, but two, bedroom scenes.

Absent is the afflicted character who gives a black lining to the comedy of certain plays. Instead, accents and linguistic fantasy proliferate. The Prince and General Koschnadieff speak with accents, and occasionally employ their own national language, an invention of the author. Van Putzeboum is the butt of witticisms as he bungles through French with his Dutch accent and ungallic constructions. Most amusing, however, is Pochet, Amélie's father, creator of magnificently complicated word clusters, malapropisms, and incredibly incorrect constructions. When Etienne interrupts his remonstrances with Amélie, who has just struck her young brother, Pochet turns to him, saying:

> Monsieur Etienne, I'm conversing to my daughter; please have the case of not inserting yourself in our intestinal discussions. When you're arguing with Amélie, I have that of not sticking a word in, don't I? Well, please have that of doing the same.
>
> (I, III)

In the estimation of a number of critics, *Occupe-toi d'Amélie* is Feydeau's masterpiece, combining the humor of *La Dame de chez Maxim* and the psychological truth of *Le Dindon*. Everywhere in this play, even at the most preposterous moments, Feydeau's astute powers of observation are in evidence. In the masterly opening scene we are taken behind the scenes in the world of the *cocotte* and witness a light-hearted gathering of the demimonde. The famous marriage scene of Act III contains a biting caricature of social institutions, while the final scene reveals the dishonesty and bad faith of the police.

Selfishness, pettiness, fatuousness, rapacity and ambition are everywhere in evidence. Yet in this carefree world no one seems to suffer too much from the vices of others. Even Etienne, angered at first by Marcel's betrayal of his trust, derives pleasure from his revenge. Amélie herself, so much less grasping and selfish than the others, has used the needs of men to achieve her present position. With charming ingenuousness and comic frankness she admits it to her former employer, the Comtesse du Prémilly (Irène), who has recognized her as her former chambermaid:

> IRÈNE, *commiseratingly*: So, you've become . . .
> AMÉLIE, *as though the most natural thing in the world*: A cocotte, yes, madame.
> IRÈNE: Oh! But how could you have fallen . . .
> AMÉLIE: Ambition! . . . I had it in the back of my mind. I just wasn't made to be a chambermaid.
>
> (I, VII)

In a day when 100 performances was considered a long run, *Occupe-toi d'Amélie* chalked up 255. It was one of Armande Cassive's greatest personal triumphs. After a number of revivals, *Amélie* was absent from Paris theaters for almost twenty years when Jean-Louis

Barrault revived it in 1948. Starring Barrault's wife, Madeleine Renaud, this production was the first important post World War II performance of Feydeau, and a revelation of unsuspected dimensions in this master of mirth. Barrault's highly-praised presentation signaled the beginning of Feydeau's ascent to classic status, consecrated by the entry of *Le Dindon* into the Comédie-Française repertoire in 1951.

Amélie had been performed on Broadway as early as 1920, under the title *Breakfast in Bed*. The year after Barrault's revival, it was made into a film, *Oh Amelia!* Noel Coward adapted it as *Look After Lulu*, a production in which "Vivien Leigh frisked about the stage of the New Theatre in her underclothes for several prosperous months," in 1959. The same adaptation, starring Tammy Grimes and Roddy McDowell, failed that year in New York. Kenneth Tynan blamed the fiasco on Coward's adaptation, Cyril Ritchard's too cute direction in a stylized burlesque, and Cecil Beaton's costumes which smothered the actors.

The currently available English version, *Keep An Eye on Amélie*, also errs on the side of cuteness. English speaking audiences have not yet seen this work in the same light that Feydeau wrote it. Indeed, almost all his plays performed in English are stylized into a kind of comedy ballet which American and English directors apparently conceive of as possessing the "Gallic touch." In France, Feydeau, despite a frenetic rhythm and the theatrical inclinations of every Frenchman, is invariably played in a fundamentally realistic style. For the foreigner, he represents (erroneously) "French bedroom farce." For the Frenchman, he stands for life itself.

Feu la mère de madame, 1908
(*Madam's Late Mother*)

Feydeau's first one-act comedy in his more sober mature style takes place in a bedroom, but it is a bedroom with a difference. No longer the center of sexual pleasures or the crossroads of frantic activity, it has become the scene of bitter quarrels and misunderstandings. Introduced in a major play as early as 1894 (*L'Hôtel du Libre-Echange*), the pessimistic picture of married life (and here, after only two years) occupies almost the entire act. No longer do we follow the complicated intrigues of wives intent on avenging themselves, or husbands on the prowl. Husbands are still prowling, and wives are still vindictive, but here, as in the four other plays which Feydeau had intended to publish in a volume to be called *From Marriage to Divorce*, the venomous dose is concentrated in a pair of portraits unrelieved by frothy plot.

It is four in the morning, and Yvonne is fast asleep when the doorbell rings. It is Lucien, her husband, who enters, ridiculously attired as Louis XIV, the Sun King (with this rain, it's absurd, the irritated wife observes). He has just returned from the Four Arts Ball, and Yvonne finds it difficult to forgive him the desertion, even more so when he attempts to explain that he has gone for artistic reasons. An amateur painter, he has been able to admire models served up stark naked. Yvonne does not share his enthusiasm, particularly when he makes clear that the models' breasts were more admirable than hers. In a hilarious scene, she opens her nightgown and makes him examine her breasts—but "Don't touch!" she admonishes—and calls the maid in to bear witness to their firmness and shapeliness.

Impatient, pitiless, unforgiving, Yvonne is wounded in her pride, and claims she will save her breasts for those who are able to appreciate them—her own version of the cry of vengeance uttered by earlier wives. When Lucien refuses to sleep in his own bed, since the maid had been sleeping there to be near her mistress, Yvonne tells him that even if he sleeps with her, he can expect nothing from her that night: "You're not going to go out and get excited looking at other women, and then come home and expect me to . . ."

Having exhausted the subject of their sexual misunderstandings, Yvonne attacks Lucien for his ways with money, defending her own spending. When finally they are both too exhausted, they go to bed, only to be roused by the doorbell. This time it is the new valet of Yvonne's mother who has come to announce the death of madame. "What a catastrophe!" cries Lucien. "Just when we were going to sleep."

When Yvonne recovers from her faint, Lucien attempts to console her, and for a moment the two are united by Yvonne's sorrow. Soon Lucien is secretly rejoicing, and while Yvonne dresses to go immediately to her mother's, Lucien writes a letter promising to pay the upholsterer who has been nagging him.

When the valet finally mentions the name of the people to whom he had come to announce the sad news, it is the name of the couple across the hall. Yvonne is overjoyed that someone else's mother has died, and Lucien upset that he has already sent off the letter to the upholsterer. "It's just like your mother to play a trick like that on us," cries Lucien, and the curtain falls on the shouts of Yvonne accusing her husband of wishing for her mother's death, and of calling her breasts traveling bags. Lucien, shouting "Shut up! Shut up!" goes off to sleep in his own dirtied bed.

Although intrigue is lacking, there is plenty of movement in *Feu la mère de madame*, and one feels the certain hand of the practiced *metteur en scène* as the author indicates in minute detail the set, movement and sometimes the intonation. Like the plays of Ionesco, which Feydeau foreshadows in more ways than one, this scene begins in relative calm—after all, Yvonne is asleep—and rises to a paroxysm of hatred and recrimination at the end. Unlike the more modern author's one-act plays, however, this one is very closely controlled, and the element of fantasy only enters in the deftest of touches. Never do we feel that the characters stand for anything more than themselves—and us, or at least our neighbors.

Although Lucien is shown as the long suffering husband, he is not entirely without blame and we cannot disagree with Yvonne when she accuses him of deserting her for the ball after only two years of marriage. Nor is she entirely unjustified in her anger at his too forthright commentary on her bosom as compared to that of the model. Lucien is, like the other males who fill Feydeau's theater, selfish, thoughtless, an ordinary person who would like to think he is quite special. Even though he has never sold a painting, he considers himself an artist.

The Louis XIV costume adds a theatrical dimension, and stresses the absurdity of Lucien's artistic pretensions. They are matched, however, by Yvonne's egotism, and blindness to her own obsession with criticizing. In her own way, she dramatizes each situation, whether storming across the room to grab her husband and show him her breasts, or playing to the hilt the role of the suffering daughter who has just lost her mother.

The violence of Yvonne's behavior, the constant movement of the stage action, the German accent of the sleepy maid, Annette, and the none too bright replies of the valet Joseph are reminders of the *vaudevilles*, as is the mistake which leads to the action in the second half of the play. Like the other techniques used with such brilliance in the more extravagant plays, this *quiproquo* also muted and used in this comedy of character to bring into relief Yvonne's and Lucien's conjugal antagonisms.

The esteem in which the French hold this play is reflected by its inclusion in the Comédie-Française's repertoire since 1941. It was the first Feydeau play to be performed at the prestigious First Theater of France.

On purge bébé, 1910
(*Going to Pot*)

One of Feydeau's most acid comedies, *On purge bébé* is also one of the funniest. It is difficult to avoid seeing it as autobiographical, for it was written shortly before the dramatist left his own home to settle in a hotel for the rest of his sane life. Indeed, his son, Jacques, has confided, "I was the hero of *On purge bébé*, and things happened more or less as they do in the play."[1]

The portrait of the shrewish wife is a masterly creation, at once amusing and frightening in the egotism, selfishness and blindness it reveals. Self-righteous and firm in her motherly and wifely convictions, Julie is the incarnation of bad faith. Her contradictory behavior, illogical thinking, and passionate outbursts suggest a mental imbalance sufficient to unhinge the stoutest husband. The simple situation, stress on character study, and physiological detail are typical of Naturalistic plays, but the tone, and occasionally the absurd exaggeration, remain close to that of Feydeau's

179

vaudeville. Here, however, they are darkened by the personal tragedies of the author, apparently paralleling in some ways those of the husband in *On purge bébé*.

Follavoine is expecting Monsieur Chouilloux, an employee of the Ministry of War, for lunch. He looks forward to winning from him a contract to supply the entire French army with individual chamber pots. Since Follavoine is in the porcelain business, such a large contract would make his fortune. He is all the more upset, therefore, when his wife, Julie, appears shortly before noon with her hair still up, her stockings round her ankles, and her nightgown hanging below an unkempt dressing gown. Despite all his urging, she insists upon arguing with him over every statement he makes. They bicker childishly over who found the word Hebrides in the dictionary under the letter H, after having vainly searched for it under several erroneous spellings. Her clothing, other women, her family, her mother, and most of all, Toto, their seven-year-old son, preoccupy the prattling and fussing of Julie.

Nothing the husband says is right. If he speaks of Julie's mother as "my mother-in-law," Julie accuses him of being unkind and cruel. If he excuses the grandmother for spoiling little Toto, Julie accuses him of taking her side against his wife.

Toto, it appears, is currently constipated, and Julie, worried sick over his health, insists that Follavoine try to make him take his laxative. In the midst of this situation, Chouilloux arrives. Follavoine attempts to convince him of the superiority of his own unbreakable porcelain chamber pots, but has no success in proving their unbreakability, since the two he throws across the room are smashed to pieces.

When Julie erupts into the room, she is still in her

untidy garb and so preoccupied with Toto's laxative that she is grossly impolite to Chouilloux. Finally, she attempts to make Toto drink his medicine by offering to have Chouilloux drink a glass of it at the same time. The guest refuses, but when, a few minutes later, Julie unthinkingly refers to Chouilloux as a cuckold (a situation all Paris apparently knows of, only the husband remaining ignorant), he is aghast, and choking with anger, unwittingly downs the medicine, then runs off to find the nearest bathroom.

In the meantime, Mme Chouilloux and a male cousin who is her constant companion arrive, and when her husband returns and accuses his wife of adultery, Follavoine finds himself struck and challenged by both husband and cousin. Choking with anger after they storm out, Follavoine drinks the remaining glass of laxative, and himself storms out of the house, leaving Julie to hug and coo over her little Toto, who hypocritically claims he has drunk all his laxative.

Often considered one of Feydeau's masterpieces, this comedy of character reveals the dramatist's infallible eye for gesture, facial expression and manner, and his infallible ear for the patterns of middle-class speech. Blending, as Jean Anouilh was to do thirty or forty years later, the pink of comedy with the black of reality, Feydeau paints a picture of marriage as an endless struggle between two beings made never to understand each other. Rather than verbalizing the incompatibility, however, in the manner of the younger writer (born the year *On purge bébé* premiered), Feydeau reveals the impossible situation in strictly dramatic terms, and allows us to draw the cheerless conclusions.

> "*Mais n'te promène donc pas toute nue!*" 1911
> (*"Don't Walk Around Stark Naked!"*)

Like the unbearable wife in *On purge bébé*, the ingenuous spouse in this play ruins her husband's hopes for success in his career. But unlike the bitter shrew of the year before, Clarisse is innocence itself —there is a freshness and charm about her insouciance which contrasts with the cold thoughtlessness of the earlier wife. With "*Mais n'te promène donc pas toute nue!*", Feydeau returns to an earlier tone of gaiety untinged by the profound pessimism of the other short plays. Although Ventroux's life is not made easy by Clarisse, at least their life is not an acrid battle perpetuated by the wife's resentment and blindness.

Ventroux is put out with Clarisse, for she has again been walking around their apartment clad only in her slip and she has not hesitated to change garments in the presence of their thirteen-year-old son. She exhibits an incredible nonchalance in the presence of the valet Victor, as well. The valet familiarly assures the worried husband that he has seen such things before. Ventroux is particularly preoccupied since he is expecting a visit from the mayor of a small town who had been especially strong in opposing Ventroux's successful candidacy to the Chamber of Deputies.

From beginning to end, Clarisse commits one *faux pas* after another. She walks into the room where Hochepaix, the mayor, is conversing with her husband, and since her husband had asked her to be kind to this guest, she calmly asks him to sit down and continues as though she were fully dressed. She is stung by a wasp, and asks her husband to do for her what she had earlier reproached his doing for a woman with whom they were picnicking recently: suck out the poison. Only Mlle Dieumamour had been stung on the neck, whereas Clarisse's wound is on the derrière. When Ventroux refuses, in panic lest she die of poisoning, she requests the same favor of Hochepaix, then of the valet, all of whom hesitate.

When an interviewer from *Le Figaro* arrives looking for an unusual story about the popular deputy, Ventroux, Clarisse mistakes him for the doctor she has sent for, and after first surprising him by appearing in her slip, further titillates him by offering her behind to be sucked. This is accomplished before the open curtain of the window, in full view of the curious Clemenceau, who lives across the street and spends his time watching from his window. As the curtain falls, the interviewer has a juicy story, Clemenceau a tasty bit of gossip, Ventroux is aghast at what must now happen to his career, and Clarisse ingenuously waves to M. Clemenceau at his window.

Lacking the depth of the other short pieces, "*Mais n'te promène donc pas toute nue!*" is nonetheless clearly satirical in its portrait of middle-class marriage, and the selfishness, egotism and thoughtlessness of both parties to a contract which, in Clarisse's words, exists only because "We said yes in front of a fat man with a tricolor ribbon [i.e., the mayor who performs civil marriages in France]." Instead of the bitter aftertaste of the preceding two short plays, the flavor left here is piquant, somewhat in the manner of the long farces, whose complications are, however, only slightly suggested by the involvements and confusions of this late piece.

Léonie est en avance, 1911 (*Léonie Is Ahead of Time*)

Once again we witness the struggle between the sexes, but in *Léonie* it is aggravated by a case of false pregnancy. During most of the one-act play Léonie is in agony, expecting to give birth to her baby at any moment. Her parents are perturbed, since she has only been married eight months, and no one, they think, will believe that the baby was premature. As it turns out, her pregnancy was simply a "case of nerves," and her parents, after having roundly chastised their son-in-law for getting his wife in this embarrassing situation so soon, now turn upon him for failing to produce a son.

Woman's selfishness and sense of superiority are stressed as first the wife, then the mother-in-law, and finally the midwife, mistreat and scorn husband and father-in-law. Toudoux comically attempts to finish his dinner at the same time that he responds to the demands of Léonie, who insists he walk her about and press on her hands in order to ease the labor pains. He is saved by the arrival of his mother-in-law, Mme de Champrinet, who unceremoniously pushes him aside to take over his functions. Léonie, requiring that all her whims be obeyed because she is pregnant, insists that Toudoux put on his head the newly arrived chamber pot for "baby." When he finally, and furiously, accedes, she is disgusted.

The officious midwife, Mme Virtuel, arrives, sends Léonie off to bed, and takes over the operation of the household, pressing not only the servant but the unhappy husband into her service. Monsieur de Champrinet arrives, and berates his son-in-law, whom he has never liked anyway, and then joins the midwife in a supper which brings on a fit of hiccups for the two of them. In the midst of this, there is much excitement offstage, and Léonie is finally delivered of—nothing. "What can you expect of a husband who is willing to wear a chamber pot on his head?" asks Mme de Champrinet derisively. As the curtain falls, the enraged husband places the pot on his father-in-law's head.

Using traditional farcical elements (hiccups, chamber pots, physical clumsiness) and themes (the war of the sexes, the dislike of sons-in-law), Feydeau continues, although less successfully, his picture of married life begun in *Feu la mère de madame* and *On purge bébé*. As always, his sense of observation leads to a series of sharply etched characters, dominated by the overwhelming Mme Virtuel. Her use of technical vocabulary, and the ensuing misunderstandings on the part of the nonplussed Toudoux, lead to some of the most amusing scenes in the play.

But despite comic moments and the picture of married life at a particularly difficult moment, *Léonie est en avance* lacks the trenchant force of Feydeau's best work and suggests, like the play that followed it (*Je ne trompe pas mon mari*, in collaboration with René Peter, 1914), that the dramatist had almost reached the end of his brilliant inventiveness.

Hortense a dit: "Je m'en fous!" 1916
(*Hortense said, "I Don't Give
a Damn!"*)

This astringently funny one-act play is Feydeau's last dazzling gasp. In the same rapid tempo as
his earlier more complicated plays, he once again—and
more virulently than ever—paints a bleak picture of
marriage destroyed by the relentless nagging and insistent complaining of a cold and shrewish wife. *Hortense a dit*: *"Je m'en fous!"* is a Strindbergian drama of
hatred in a comic key.

The dentist, Follbraguet, is busy with his patients
when his wife storms in, demanding that he fire the
maid, Hortense, who has said to her mistress, "I don't
give a damn!" Accusing her husband of being a limp
rag, incapable of defending her honor, Marcelle threatens to leave unless Follbraguet dimisses the servant.
Interrupted time and again at his work, the desperate
dentist finally dismisses the cook as well as Hortense.
When Marcelle discovers this she again threatens to
leave, derisively saying she will leave her bed for Hor-

tense to occupy. Adrien, a manservant who plans to
marry Hortense, is insulted by this aspersion of his
fiancée's honor, and after resigning his position, tells
the dentist that he will send his seconds to arrange a
duel unless the wife apologizes to Hortense.

In a white fury, the busy dentist, bending over his
last patient whose mouth is propped open and full of
surgical preparations and dental instruments, orders his
wife to leave. She refuses, reminding him that the house
is in her name. Follbraguet throws down his instruments, turns house, office and patients over to his wife,
and stalks out. Marcelle stalks out at the same time,
abandoning the poor client in the chair, openmouthed
and helpless.

Bristling with action and sharp exchanges, this final
short comedy possesses a vigor, rhythm, and sense of
movement reminiscent of the great *vaudevilles*. Lacking their complexity, it nonetheless employs some of
the same techniques of surprise and comic language.
Most comical of all, is the transposition of the "victims
of life" in earlier plays—people afflicted with deafness,
stuttering, barking, or cleft palates—to a helpless victim, first of the dental profession, and then of the Marcelle's and Follbraguet's marital misunderstandings.

As the curtain opens, the client Vildamour is being
tortured by the dentist's drill, while Follbraguet assures him that, "This doesn't hurt." Returning in the
final scene because his tooth is still aching, Vildamour
is pushed and scratched by Follbraguet in his rising ire,
and finally abandoned in the chair. Attempting to speak,
he reminds us of Camille in *La Puce à l'oreille*. But
Vildamour will presumably be cured—if he is ever
able to get the dental materials out of his mouth. Inno-

cent victim of human thoughtlessness, afflicted by man rather than some cruel fate, he finds himself in a nightmarish situation which—like that of Follbraguet himself—is familiar to every viewer.

CONCLUSION: THE MORAL
OF THE TALE

Feydeau's theater blends a varied array of comic techniques with the study of manners, deft touches of truthful characterization, and an overview which can be called metaphysical. Using theatrical languages, oral, visual, and kinesthetic, he arrives at effects that many contemporary critics have called poetic. Cocteau and the surrealists saw in him the poetry of the irrational so widely explored by the latter, and the visual poetry of the theater prescribed by the former. The French drama critic Robert Kempt compared the piling up of surprises and the abundance of episodes to the irresistible lyricism of jazz percussion, while the playwright-critic Thierry Maulnier found a kind of poetry in Feydeau's bewildering inventiveness. For actor Barrault, the dramatist endows his characters with the poetic gift of creation: through habit or distraction they make real what is only suggested, as when Amélie's father, the retired traffic policeman Pochet, transforms her apartment into a busy thoroughfare by his stern commands and admonitions.

Early achieving international popularity, Feydeau has suffered from the difficulties involved in adjusting such complex works to a foreign context. The reader or viewer who must approach his plays in English should be forewarned that what he will experience may be far from what Feydeau intended.[1]

A comparison of most recent English versions with the French originals, reveals several tendencies. For reasons not always apparent, 1) characters' names are changed, 2) nationalities are altered, and nondialect roles given dialects, 3) sex changes are effected, 4) entire passages are deleted, 5) entire passages are added, 6) unnatural plays on words and clever remarks abound, 7) a general tendency to over-cuteness prevails, 8) vulgarity is stressed, 9) songs are introduced, 10) settings are changed.

Fortunately most English versions do not commit all these sins at once. Moreover, they rarely have the effrontery to call themselves "translations." Instead, they are "adaptations" or "versions." Such transpositions are sometimes necessary, and occasionally result in a new meaningfulness totally in the spirit of Feydeau. For example, in one of the most felicitous adaptations, Suzanne Grossmann and Paxton Whitehead's *Chemin de fer* (*La Main passe*), the lover Massenay is rechristened Fédot. Among the *belle époque* audience anyone would have identified the first name with the famous composer, Jules Massenet, whereas he is unknown to large audiences today, and the translators have cleverly devised a confusion of the lover's name with that of the author himself: Fédot/Feydeau.

Comic accents in Feydeau may require a change of

nationality. An Englishwoman in an English version cannot add the same kinds of comedy that she would in a French text. Accordingly, English mistresses or governesses are often made German. John Mortimer in his version of *Un Fil à la patte* (*Cat Among the Pigeons*), turns Miss Betting into Fraulein Fitzenspiegel. Norman R. Shapiro, in his version of the same play, *Not By Bed Alone*, retains the English nationality on the grounds that only an Englishwoman fits the situation historically and socially. To bring about the necessary misunderstandings and comic effects, he makes her a mute. In this case, it strikes me that respect for sociohistorical accuracy has damaged the dramatic texture by infusing an element of pathos, and disrupted the rhythmic flow by introducing mimed segments for the deleted English dialogue.

Hotel Paradiso changes the names of Pinglet to Boniface, Paillardin to Cot, the hotel keeper from French Bastien to a thick-accented Italian Anniello, and the French student evicted from the hotel becomes a Turk with a white turban! The last two changes may add color and a certain facile humor, but certainly Feydeau was theatrically sophisticated enough to gauge the degree of color and the kind of humor best suited to each scene. Indeed, he is so insistent in his notes and stage directions regarding accurate observation of the author's wishes, that it is easy to imagine his restless ghost rising midst bedsheets and lamps, like the Môme Crevette, to take revenge upon his faithless translators.

The adaptors most certain to be singled out for such a visit are those who perpetrated *The Lady From Maxim's*. The French original is Feydeau's longest text. The English version is the shortest—about half as long as *Chemin de fer*, which in French is 30 pages shorter than *La Dame de chez Maxim*. This shortening was in part accomplished by deleting much of Acts I and III, and most of Act II, including the colorful picture of provincial manners. Equally missing are the many occasions on which Crevette utters the phrase which became famous overnight and went the rounds of all Paris, "C'est pas mon père!" As though this were not enough, whole pages of non-Feydeau repartee are introduced, cute Gilbert and Sullivan type exchanges, and all is topped off with seven songs. The one song Feydeau did include in his text is, needless to say, deleted, for it fit logically into its place. What we are confronted with is a kind of musical comedy which stands to Feydeau as *My Fair Lady* does to Shaw. The dangers of introducing extraneous songs into a Feydeau text should be pointed out, for songs destroy the all-important rhythm established in these ingeniously constructed machines where pace and rhythm are not overlooked with impunity. To throw a song into such a delicate mechanism amounts to sabotage. But *The Lady From Maxim's* in its English version is so distant from Feydeau, and its mechanism so unrefined, that the question of sabotage is irrelevant.

Difficulties of translation are perhaps compounded by the understanding of farce among English-speaking people. Feydeau is the quintessence of French farce, as it developed traditions somewhat different from those of English farce in the nineteenth century. Like all farce, Feydeau's is highly physical, delighting in chases, disguises willful or not, quick-moving appearances and disappearances, and even the "low comedy" of kicks in the pants, collapsing chairs and other embarrassing mishaps. Like other farces, his too deal with the absurd as though it were the most normal of circumstances.

Unlike most French farce before him, however, and unlike all English farce, Feydeau's plays carry both physicality and absurdity to an incredible degree of paroxism. Changing formulas, here he stresses the chase, there the mistaken identity; here the absurd of situation, there the more grim absurd of human suffering. Compared to the masterpieces of English nineteenth-century farce, any major play of Feydeau's glows with a hard, bright light which derives from its uncompromising, if somewhat disguised, attachment to truth, and from its purposeful excess in using the techniques of the genre pushed to the nth degree.

The complications and savage humor of *Champignol malgré lui* cannot even be approximated by that pleasant and most favorite of madly English farces, *Charley's Aunt*, which was its precise contemporary, both opening during the final months of 1892. The naughty intrigues and hair-raising adventures of Cis and Mr. Posket at the Hôtel des Princes in Sir Arthur Wing Pinero's run-about farce, *The Magistrate* (1885), pale in the company of Pinglet, Marcelle and Paillardin at the Hôtel du Libre-Echange. And W. S. Gilbert's enchantingly ironic *Tom Cobb* (1875), whose hero is subtitled (as any of Feydeau's might be) "Fortune's Toys," becomes artifice pure and simple when placed alongside any of Feydeau's major works.

The truth is that English farce blunted its edge with sentimentality and at least the suggestions of moralizing. Like melodrama and thesis plays in both countries, English farce affirmed the status quo and entrenched the public more securely in its comfortable beliefs. In this good homely entertainment there was no place for *cocottes*, adultresses or philandering husbands. When French *vaudevilles* were adapted for English audiences, which happened often, guilty couples were whitewashed by marriage, mistresses became girl friends, and *cocottes* were deodorized or expunged.

The traditions of French farce, unattenuated by Victorianism, allowed Feydeau to deal with the same areas of real life that were dealt with in serious drama. In England, it was apparently felt that wicked women and adultery were the province of serious theater where they could be appropriately punished. Accordingly, Pinero, England's outstanding farceur in his youth, relegated those tasty subjects to his dramas, reserving for his farces only situations which were capable of being resolved in such a way as to show that, after all, domestic joys are superior to more dazzling lures.

With the sharp-edged blade of truth, Feydeau cuts through these pious myths, suggesting that love, in or out of wedlock, is something of a disappointment. In the tradition of farce, all must end well—but, after the dizzying adventures of his "toys of fortune," we are rarely prepared to conclude that all is for the best. Happy endings in Feydeau are only temporary solutions.

They are temporary solutions because life lies at the center of Feydeau's plays. Rather than evasion into a misty world of wish-fulfilment, we are brought face to face with the absurdity of our predicament, incarnated in a mechanism of such perfection, speed, and violence that human struggle is useless. Here lies the fundamental seriousness of Feydeau. Expressed in the entire structure of his plays, his view of man's lot does not reaffirm our lazy pretenses, but serves, as all serious theater must, to raise doubts. It destroys our self-satisfaction and security, throws all into question, and by its very violence strikes deeper than more serious ideas expressed discursively might do.

In what is perhaps the best-known of all commentaries on the plays of Feydeau, Marcel Achard compares these masterpieces of vaudeville to tragedy:

> Feydeau's plays possess the progression, the force and the violence of tragedy. They possess its ineluctable fatality. Witnessing tragedy, we choke with horror. Witnessing Feydeau, we choke with laughter. Even the heroes of Shakespeare and Racine give us the respite of beautiful verse in which they melodiously express their misfortunes. Feydeau's heroes don't even have time to feel sorry for themselves, for it is characteristic of their destiny that it makes us laugh because the small catastrophe which has just barely finished opens the way to an immense annoyance which we know is only the first of a long series. Jean Cocteau claims that the gods construct highly perfected infernal machines for the annihilation of mortals. The god Feydeau ordered his from a shop selling jokes and pranks.[2]

If it is clear from a reading (or preferably, a viewing) of Feydeau's infernal machines that men are the victims of the gods, it is equally clear that men are particularly vulnerable to divine machinations because they have certain inherent weaknesses. Like the hero of classical tragedy led by hubris to match himself against a force which is greater than he, Feydeau's weak mortals are usually responsible for their own catastrophes. Unheroically, they are unaware of pitting themselves against unbeatable odds, for they rarely suffer from lucidity. It is *we* who gain lucidity from contemplation of their woes.

Bouzin (*Un Fil à la patte*) hopes to profit from the anonymous bouquet left for Lucette, and drops his own card into it, thereby loosening on himself the fury of the gods—or at least that of the jealous Latin American general—and spends the rest of the play fleeing, not sure just why. Pontagnac (*Le Dindon*), prompted by the demon of lust (or simply habit), dares to enter an honest woman's home in pursuit of her; this insistence results in the loss of his own wife, and leaves him holding nothing but the bag. Dr. Petypon (*La Dame de chez Maxim*) spent a night on the town and finds la Môme Crevette inextricably wedged into his life. Marcel (*Occupe-toi d'Amélie*) did the same and ultimately finds himself married to the wrong woman.

Through blindness, foolishness, stupidity, weakness, selfishness, avarice, and other human foibles, Feydeau's characters set off the machinery that will trap them. The moral of the tale—if moral there is—would appear to be that we foolish mortals are not entirely innocent. Shocked and amazed, we look at the shambles of our lives, not realizing that it is we who have brought the whole structure tumbling about our ears.

And yet, modern in its ambiguity, this theater also shows us victims who are innocent: deaf old Mme Pinchard, Paillardin who only went to the Hôtel du Libre-Echange in a professional capacity; Chandebise who goes to the Hôtel du Minet Galant to warn his friends of impending danger. Foolish or smart, selfish or altruistic, guilty or innocent: all are condemned. The world of Feydeau *is* the world of the Absurd in which man is invariably pitted against forces that resist his search for happiness and meaning, and rarely allow him to attain even the more realistic goals of peace and pleasure.

This bitter lucidity which pierces the frenzied running around, and the violent energy which emerges from such a paradoxical encounter, make Feydeau excruciatingly modern. They explain in large part his immense appeal today to audiences, actors, directors and critics alike.

In a precise way, Feydeau's characters embody the definition Camus gave of absurdity. It is not man that is absurd, he claimed. Nor is it the universe. Absurdity lies precisely in the meeting of these two: men with their hopes, dreams and needs placed in a blind, silent, meaningless universe. Indeed, in Feydeau man seems so ill-fitted to his habitat that one sometimes feels the universe is quite actively inimical, pulling the carpet out from under the feet of unsuspecting mortals. This is the vision so clearly sensed by Thierry Maulnier when he witnessed the Comédie-Française revival of *Le Dindon* in 1951:

> How could one help feeling without an almost unbearable anguish the call which emanates from Feydeau's creatures, a cry of accusation against a universe where man himself, with his wish for reason and happiness, is the most irreparable absurdity?[3]

Like some spastic Sisyphus chasing a stone uphill only to see it roll down again, Feydeau's characters—like ourselves—are caught on the treadmill of absurdity.

NOTES

Georges Feydeau and *La Belle Epoque*

1. Introduction to Georges Feydeau, *Théâtre complet*, Paris, Le Bélier, 1948. Volume I, p. 7. An English version, with some inaccuracies, appears in *Let's Get a Divorce! and Other Plays*, edited by Eric Bentley, New York, Hill and Wang, 1958.
2. Louis Verneuil, *Rideau à neuf heures*, New York, Editions de la Maison Française, Inc., 1944, p. 95.
3. *Ibid.*
4. René Peter, *Le Théâtre et la vie sous la Troisième République*, Paris, Editions Marchot, 1947. Volume II, footnote, pp. 37–38. There are several versions of this story.
5. Quoted by Marcel Achard, *op. cit.*, p. 10.
6. Quoted in Gilbert Guilleminault, *Prélude à la Belle Epoque*, Paris, Editions Denoël, 1956, p. 115.

The Geometry of Madness

1. Léon Treich, "Le 10e anniversaire de la mort de Feydeau," quoted in Arlette Shenkan, *Georges Feydeau*, Paris, Seghers, 1972, p. 156.
2. Adolphe Brisson, "Une Leçon de vaudeville," quoted in Arlette Shenkan, *ibid.*, p. 152.
3. Arlette Shenkan, *Georges Feydeau*, Paris, Seghers, 1972, p. 153.
4. Adolphe Brisson, *ibid.*, p. 151.
5. Leon Treich, *op. cit.*, p. 155.
6. René Peter, *Le Théâtre et la vie sous la Troisième République*, Volume II, Paris, Editions Marchot, 1947, p. 240.
7. Henri Bergson, *Le Rire*, Paris, Presses Universitaires, 1947, p. 78.
8. Henri Jeanson, "Notes sur Georges Feydeau," *Cahiers de la Compagnie Madeleine Renaud-Jean-Louis Barrault*, No. 32, Dec., 1960, p. 20.

The Taste for Truth

1. The date usually given is 1887. In his article, "Georges Feydeau: une date essentielle corrigée," (*Revue d'histoire du théâtre*, Oct.-Dec., 1962, pp. 362-364), Norman R. Shapiro shows without any doubt that the play was actually performed a year earlier. André Antoine's year-by-year listing of Paris theater performances *Le Théâtre*, (Paris, Les Editions de France, 1932), supports his conclusions.
2. René Peter, *Le Théâtre et la vie sous la Troisième République*, Volume II, Paris, Editions Marchot, 1947, p. 241.
3. Jean-Louis Barrault, *Souvenirs pour demain*, Paris, Editions du Seuil, 1972, p. 201.

The Plays

1. Jacques Lorcey, *Georges Feydeau*, Paris, La Table Ronde, 1972, p. 203.

Conclusion: The Moral of the Tale

1. Some of the problems encountered by the translator are discussed in the preface to Norman R. Shapiro, *Four Farces by George Feydeau*, pp. ix-xi.
2. Introduction to Georges Feydeau, *Théâtre complet*, Volume I, Paris, Le Bélier, 1948, p. 18. An English translation is found in *Let's Get a Divorce! and Other Plays*, edited by Eric Bentley, New York, Hill and Wang, 1958.
3. "La Querelle du *Dindon*," *Combat*, March 9, 1951. Quoted in Shenkan, *Georges Feydeau*, pp. 162-163.

BIBLIOGRAPHY

I. Plays of Georges Feydeau

All of the following plays are contained in the nine volumes of Feydeau's *Théâtre complet*, Paris, Editions du Bélier, 1948–1956. The title is followed by a literal translation in parentheses, a Roman numeral referring to the volume of the *Théâtre complet* in which it is found, the date of its first performance, and other known but unpublished titles for the play. Published versions are listed separately below the entry in French.

Par la fenêtre (Through the Window), IV, 1881.
　Wooed and Viewed, tr. by Norman R. Shapiro,
　Four Farces by Georges Feydeau. Chicago, U. of
　Chicago Press, 1970.
Amour et piano (Love and Piano), I, 1883.
Gibier de potence (Gallows-bird), VI, 1884.
Fiancés en herbe (Unripe fiancés), I, 1886.
Tailleur pour dames (Ladies' Tailor), IX, 1886.

A Gown for His Mistress, tr. Barnett Shaw, New York, Samuel French,

La Lycéenne (The Schoolgirl), VIII, 1887.

Un Bain de ménage (Household Bath), VII, 1888.

Chat en poche (A Bird in Hand), II, 1888.

Les Fiancés de Loches (The Fiancés from Loches), with M. Desvallières, VII, 1888.

L'Affaire Edouard (The Edward Affair), with M. Desvallières, I, 1889.

C'est une femme du monde (She's a Lady of Quality), with M. Desvallières, IV, 1890.

Le Mariage de Barillon (Barillon's Marriage), with M. Desvallières, V, 1890.
  On The Marry-Go-Wrong, tr. by Norman R. Shapiro, *Four Farces by Georges Feydeau*. Chicago, U. of Chicago Press, 1970.

Monsieur chasse (Master Is Hunting), V, 1892.
  The Happy Hunter, tr. by Barnett Shaw, New York, Samuel French, 1973.
  13 Rue de l'Amour, tr. by Mawby Green and Ed Feilbert, New York, Samuel French, 1972.

Champignol malgré lui (Champignol in Spite of Himself), with M. Desvallières, VI, 1892.

Le Système Ribadier (The Ribadier System), II, 1892.

Un Fil à la patte (Tied by the Leg), VI, 1894. The Lady from Lobster Square.
  Cat Among the Pigeons, tr. by John Mortimer, New York, Samuel French, 1970.
  Not By Bed Alone, tr. by Norman R. Shapiro, *Four Farces by Georges Feydeau*, Chicago, U. of Chicago Press, 1970.

Notre futur (Our Intended), VI, 1894.

Le Ruban (The Decoration), VIII, 1894.

L'Hôtel du Libre-Echange (Free Exchange Hotel), with M. Desvallières, IV, 1894.
  Hotel Paradiso, tr. by Peter Glenville, New York, Samuel French, 1958.

Le Dindon (The Dupe), II, 1896. There's One in Every Marriage.

Les Pavés de l'ours (Save Me from My Friends), II, 1896.

Séance de nuit (Night Session), II, 1897.

Dormez, je le veux! (Sleep, I command it!), III, 1897.

La Dame de chez Maxim (The Lady from Maxim's), VII, 1899. The Girl from Montmartre.
   The Lady from Maxim's, tr. by Gene Feist, New York, Samuel French, 1971.

La Duchesse des Folies Bergère (The Duchess from the Folies Bergère), VIII, 1902.

La Main passe (Your Deal Next), III, 1904. The Chemmy Circle.
   Chemin de fer, tr. by Suzanne Grossmann and Paxton Whitehead, New York, Samuel French, 1968.

L'Age d'or (The Golden Age), with M. Desvallières, IX, 1905.

Le Bourgeon (The Sprout), IX, 1906.

La Puce à l'oreille (A Flea in Her Ear), IV, 1970.
   A Flea in Her Ear, tr. by Barnett Shaw, New York, Samuel French, available in manuscript only.
   A Flea in Her Ear, tr. by John Mortimer, London, Samuel French Ltd., 1968.

Occupe-toi d'Amélie (Take Care of Amélie), I, 1908. Breakfast in Bed.
   Keep an Eye on Amélie, tr. by Brainerd Duffield, in *Let's Get a Divorce! and Other Plays,* New York, Hill and Wang, 1958.
   Look After Lulu, tr. by Noel Coward, New York, Samuel French, 1959.

Feu la mère de madame (Madam's Late Mother), VII, 1908.

Le Circuit (The Road Race), with Francis de Croisset, V, 1909.

On purge bébé (Purging Baby), III, 1910.
   Going to Pot, tr. by Norman R. Shapiro, *Four*

Farces by Georges Feydeau, Chicago, U. of Chicago Press, 1970. This translation also appears in *Tulane Drama Review*, Autumn, 1960.

"*Mais n'te promène donc pas toute nue!*" ("Don't Walk Around Stark Naked!"), VIII, 1911.

Léonie est en avance (Léonie is Ahead of Time), IV, 1911.

Je ne trompe pas mon mari (I'm Not Deceiving My Husband), with René Peter, III, 1914.

Hortense a dit: "Je m'en fous!" (Hortense Said, "I Don't Give A Damn!"), I, 1916.

Cent millions qui tombent (A Hundred Million Landfall), VI, unfinished.

On va faire la cocotte (We're Going to Play at Tarts), VII, unfinished.

II. SELECTED CRITICISM

In French

Barrault, Jean-Louis, *et al.,* `Cahiers de la Compagnie Madeleine Renaud-Jean-Louis Barrault*, No. 32, Dec., 1960, "La Question Feydeau."

Brisson, Adolphe, *Portraits intimes*, Volume V, Paris, Armand Colin, 1901.

Lorcey, Jacques, *Georges Feydeau*, Paris, La Table Ronde, 1972.

Shenkan, Arlette, *Georges Feydeau*, Paris, Seghers, 1972.

Treich, Leon, *L'Esprit de Georges Feydeau*, Paris, Gallimard, 1927.

In English

Anonymous, "Forms of Shock Treatment for a World Out of Plumb," *Times Literary Supplement*, 18 June, 1971, pp. 689-690. (Review of Norman R. Shapiro's *Four Farces by Georges Feydeau*.)

Bentley, Eric, editor, *Let's Get a Divorce! and Other Plays.* New York, Hill and Wang, 1958. Introduction, Note, and Appendix (Marcel Achard's "Georges Feydeau").

Shapiro, Norman R., "Suffering and Punishment in the Theatre of Georges Feydeau," *The Tulane Drama Review*, Volume 5, No. 1, September, 1960, pp. 117-126.

Shapiro, Norman R., "Introduction," in *Four Farces by Georges Feydeau*, Chicago, U. of Chicago Press, 1970.

INDEX

Absurd, elements of the, 7,
    26, 29–30, 38, 63, 64,
    74, 75, 89, 90, 101,
    107, 115, 121, 147,
    164, 178, 179, 194–
    95, 196, 198, 199
Absurd, Theater of the, 20,
    50, 98–99, 149
Achard, Marcel, 6, 140, 197
Action, use of, 31–34, 36,
    40–41, 113, 178, 189
Adultery theme, 57, 67, 73,
    89, 91, 96, 146, 171
Affaire Edouard, L', 28, 57
Afternoon of a Faun, The
    (Debussy), 18
Age d'or, L', 26
American productions of
    plays, 81, 84, 86, 99,
    115, 122, 130, 151,
    165, 174
Amour et piano, 7–8, 47
Anouilh, Jean, 72, 130, 181
Antoine, André, 24, 25, 52,
    53, 65, 108
Apollinaire, Guillaume, 18,
    19
Artaud, Antonin, 74
Aside, use of, 8, 89, 143
Augier, Emile, 22, 24, 70
Autobiographical elements,
    10, 179, 180
Avare, L' (Molière), 27

Bald Soprano, The
    (Ionesco), 99
Barrault, Jean-Louis, 55, 79,
    173–74, 191
Beaton, Cecil, 174
Beckett, Samuel, 50
Becque, Henri, 66, 72–73
Belle époque, 12–15, 17–19,
    20, as setting, 5, 53–54
Belle Otero, La, 14
Bergson, Henri, 18, 43, 44,
    46–47, 49, 50
Bernhardt, Sarah, 18, 23,
    24, 25
Black humor, 26, 181
Blériot, Louis, 17
Boileau, Nicolas, 22
Boubouroche (Courteline),
    65
Boulevard theater, 6, 9, 21,
    24, 25, 52
Bourgeois gentilhomme, Le
    (Molière), 27
Bourgeoisie, portrayal of,
    5, 13, 19–20, 37, 53,
    58, 66, 69, 98, 114,
    121, 131, 143, 150,
    154, 163, 166, 181,
    183–84
Bourgeon, Le, 26, 29, 58,
    70, 123, 152–56, 166
Braque, Georges, 17
Breakfast in Bed (Occupe-

toi d'Amélie), 28, 32, 36, 40, 46, 48, 55, 57, 58, 79, 166–74, 198
British productions of plays, 115, 122, 165, 174

Café-concerts, 12
Café Weber, 12–13
Caillaux, Mme, 19
Camus, Albert, 199
Cantatrice chauve, La (Ionesco), 99
Caricature, use of, 173
Cassive, Armande, 143–44, 173
Castellane, Count Boni de, 15
Cat Among the Pigeons (*Un Fil à la patte*), 15, 28, 36, 41, 45, 46, 85, 109–115, 130, 142, 193, 198
Catholic Church, 5, 141–42
Champignol malgré lui, 9, 28, 36, 44–45, 47, 76, 91, 101–108, 195
Champion, Gower, 86, 165
Chaplin, Charlie, 50
Character, comedies of, 10, 26, 27, 36–37, 42, 48–49, 65, 68, 130, 178, 181
Characterization, 8, 13, 28, 33, 34, 66, 67, 90, 93, 107, 114, 121, 141,

149, 150, 155, 156, 164, 175, 177, 186, 191, 197–98, 199
of afflicted persons, 60–64, 114, 121, 131, 141, 147, 149, 150, 158, 163–64, 172, 189
of aristocracy, 58, 154
of *cocottes*, 36, 45, 54–55, 59, 109, 114, 132, 153, 166, 173
of foreigners, 60
of men, 98, 116, 130, 177–78, 197
of the military, 59, 103, 108
of professionals, 55–58
of provincial society, 58–59, 135
of servants, 59–60, 89
of women, 10, 68, 70, 89, 98, 124, 160, 179, 182, 185, 188
See also Bourgeoisie, portrayal of
Charley's Aunt (English farce), 195
Chase, use of, 114–15, 194, 195
Chat en poche, 30, 47
Chemin de fer (*La Main passe*), 28, 45, 50, 57, 66–67, 70, 84, 145–51, 156, 166, 192
Circuit, Le, 26–27
Claudel, Paul, 18, 29

212 | INDEX

Clouard, Henri (quoted), 120–21
Cocottes, 13–15
Cocteau, Jean, 35, 50, 151, 191, 197
Coincidence, use of, 34, 38, 48, 97, 107, 120, 155
Colette, 18
Collaborations, 8–9, 29, 42, 54, 116, 187
Comédie-Française, 54, 83, 85, 115, 129, 130, 164, 174, 178, 199
Comedies of manners, 22, 130, 135, 141, 145, 163, 167, 191, 194
Comedy, classical, 44, 45
Comic techniques, 29–31, 42–49, 88–89, 97–98, 114, 120, 123, 141, 142, 150, 178, 186, 189, 191, 194–95
Compagnie Grenier-Hussenot, 122
Coquelin, Benoît Constant, 24
Corbeaux, Les (Becque), 66
Corbière, Tristan, 62
Coups de théâtre, 30–31, 124
Courteline, Georges, 12, 64–65
Coward, Noel, 174
Cubism, 17
Curel, François de, 152
Curie, Pierre and Marie, 17

Cyrano de Bergerac (Rostand), 18, 24, 25

Dame aux camélias, La (Dumas the younger), 28–29, 114
Dame de chez Maxim, La, 13, 19, 28, 35, 36, 37, 39–40, 45–46, 55–56, 58–59, 121, 132–44, 172, 193–94, 198
Debussy, Claude, 18
Deception theme, 28–29, 33, 41, 46
Demi-monde theme, 8, 13–14, 114, 166, 173
Derain, André, 17
Desvallières, Maurice, 8–9, 29, 116
Dialogues, 26
Dindon, Le, 25, 28, 29, 46, 48, 56–57, 59, 61–62, 69, 70–71, 85, 123–31, 140, 142, 145, 156, 172–73, 174, 198, 199
Donnay, Maurice, 29
Dormez, je le veux!, 45, 59–60
Dramas, 26, 29, 70, 152
Drame, device of, 34
Dreyfus affair, 18–19, 141
Duchesse des Folies-Bergères, La, 28, 58
Dumas the elder, 22
Dumas the younger, 22, 24, 28–29, 52, 70, 123–24, 152, 154–55

Edward VII of England, 15
Eiffel Tower, 17
Existentialism, 20

Fanny (E. Feydeau), 6
Farce, 7, 9, 52, 63, 143, 157,
    194–96
  bedroom farce, 5–6, 172
  techniques of, 8, 48, 74,
      89, 91, 98, 114, 121,
      142, 152, 156, 186
Faure, Félix, 19
Feu la mère de madame, 26,
    67–68, 82, 130, 175–
    78, 186
Feydeau, Ernest (father), 6
Feydeau, Georges
  acting career of, 7
  childhood of, 6
  directing career of, 32,
      143, 166, 177
  laziness of, 6–7, 166
  life style of, 10–13, 15–16
  marriage of, 7, 10, 179
  melancholia of, 10, 11
Feydeau, Jacques (son),
    179
Feydeau, Marianne (wife),
    7, 10
Fiancés de Loches, Les, 29,
    47, 56
Fil à la patte, Un, 15, 28, 36,
    41, 45, 46, 85, 109–
    115, 130, 142, 193,
    198
Film versions of plays, 122,
    165, 174

Finney, Albert, 165
Flea in Her Ear, A (La
    Puce a l'oreille), 7,
    28, 36, 37, 41, 45, 48,
    56, 63, 71–73, 80, 81,
    86, 142, 157–65, 166,
    190
Flers, Robert de (quoted),
    11
Franco-Prussian war, 18
French art and literature,
    17–18
French theater, 7, 21–25,
    152, 163
From Marriage to Divorce,
    175

Gadgets, use of, 142
Gaîté parisienne (Offen-
    bach), 18
Gide, André, 18
Gilbert, W. S., 195
Going to Pot (On purge
    bébé), 26, 57, 67,
    140, 179–81, 182, 186
Gould, Anna, 15
Gown for His Mistress, A
    (Tailleur pour
    dames), 8, 24, 28, 45,
    53, 55, 76–90
Grimes, Tammy, 174
Grossmann, Suzanne, 192
Guinness, Alec, 122

Happy Hunter, The
    (Monsieur chasse),
    9, 28, 57, 91–100

Haussman, Baron, 12, 18
Hennequin, Alfred, 9
Herne, James A., 29
Hervieu, Paul, 29
History of Burial Customs and Graves Among the Ancients (E. Feydeau), 6
History of French Literature (Clouard), 120–21
Hortense a dit: "Je m'en fous!" 56, 67, 188–90
Hôtel du Libre-Echange, L', 8, 28, 37, 43, 45, 56, 57, 68–69, 83, 116–22, 175, 193
Hotel Paradiso. See: L'Hôtel du Libre-Echange
Hotel Terminus, life at, 10, 16
Hugo, Victor, 22, 24, 34

Ibsen, Henrik, 18, 22
Idées de Madame Aubray, Les (Dumas), 124, 155
Imagery, use of, 68
Imbroglio. *See* Action, use of
Interference of series, device of, 44, 46–48
Inversion, device of, 44, 45–46, 88–89
Ionesco, Eugène, 50, 61, 74, 99, 121, 177

Jarry, Alfred, 18, 25, 69
Jeanmaire, Zizi, 140
Je ne trompe pas mon marie, 27, 42, 187
Jones, Henry Arthur, 29

Kafka, Franz, comparison with, 50, 113
Keep an Eye on Amélie (Occupe-toi d'Amélie), 28, 32, 36, 40, 46, 48, 55, 57, 58, 79, 166–74, 198
Kempt, Robert, 191

Labiche, Eugène, 9, 26
Lady from Lobster Square, The (Un Fil à la patte), 15, 28, 36, 41, 45, 46, 85, 109–115, 130, 142, 193, 198
Lady from Maxim's, The (La Dame de chez Maxim), 13, 19, 28, 35, 36, 37, 39–40, 45–46, 55–56, 58–59, 121, 132–44, 172, 193–94, 198
Lahr, Bert, 122
Language, comic use of, 8, 16, 42–44, 54–55, 58, 60–61, 63, 107, 114, 167, 172, 181, 186, 189, 192–93
Leigh, Vivien, 174
Léonie est en avance, 67–68, 185–87

Letter, device of, 163
Libertinage, element of, 31
Look After Lulu
	(Coward), 174
Lorenzaccio (Musset), 24
Love, theme of, 8, 66, 69–
	70, 70–71, 72–73, 121,
	124, 130, 150, 196
Lugné-Poë, Alexandre, 24
Lycéenne, La, 26

Machine infernale, La
	(Cocteau), 35
Maeterlinck, Maurice, 24–
	25
Magistrate, The (Pinero),
	195
Main passe, La, 28, 45, 50,
	57, 66–67, 70, 84,
	145–51, 156, 166, 192
"*Mais n'te promène donc
	pas toute nue!*" 26,
	57, 83, 182–84
Malapropism, use of, 58,
	167, 172
Manners, comedies of, 22,
	130, 135, 141, 145,
	163, 167, 191, 194
Mariage de Barillon, Le, 57
Marriage theme, 8, 10, 26,
	38, 65, 66, 67, 68–69,
	70, 98, 108, 114, 121,
	124, 130, 145, 150–
	51, 166, 175, 181,
	183–84, 186, 188, 196
Massenet, Jules, 192
Materialism theme, 114, 121

Matisse, Henri, 17
Maulnier, Thierry, 191, 199
Mauvais bergers, Les
	(Mirabeau), 25
Maxim's restaurant, 12, 13,
	14, 166
McDowell, Roddy, 174
Meilhac, Henri, 9
Melodrama, 31, 34, 163
Mendès, Catulle, 12
Metaphysical dimension, 5,
	20, 21, 33, 50, 64, 65,
	75, 90, 191, 196–97
Mirabeau, Octave, 25
Molière, 6, 27, 54, 135, 140,
	143
Monde, le, 14
Monologues, 7
Monsieur chasse, 9, 28, 57,
	91–100
Mortimer, John, 115, 193
Mounet-Sully, 18, 24
Movement, theatrical, 32,
	38–40, 41, 98, 115,
	123, 149, 177, 178
Music, use of, 26, 89, 194
Musical comedy, 22
Music halls, 12, 89
Musset, Alfred de, 24, 194

Names, comic use of, 88
Napolitain café, 12
Naturalism movement, 18,
	24, 25, 31, 50, 52, 53,
	64–66, 108, 163, 179
Nijinsky, Vaslaw, 17

Not By Bed Alone (*Un Fil à la patte*), 15, 28, 36, 41, 45, 46, 85, 109–115, 130, 142, 193, 198

"Obligatory scene" (*scène à faire*), 23, 35, 40, 155
Observation, use of, 31, 51, 53, 98, 173, 181, 186
Occupe-toi d'Amélie, 28, 32, 36, 40, 46, 48, 55, 57, 58, 79, 166–74, 198
Odéon theater, 83, 129, 130
Oeuvre of Feydeau, 26–27
Offenbach, Jacques, 18
Oh Amélie!, 174
Olivier, Laurence, 165
One-act plays, 26, 175, 185, 188
On purge bébé, 26, 57, 67, 140, 179–81, 182, 186

Palais-Royal theater, 9, 91, 101
Panama scandal, 18
Pantomime, use of, 149
Paris, of *belle époque*, 12–13, 17, 18
Parisienne, La (Becque), 66
Partage de midi, Le (Claudel), 29
Péguy, Charles, 18
Pelléas et Mélisande (Debussy), 18

Pelléas et Mélisande (Maeterlinck), 24–25
Pessimism, 131, 175, 182
Peter, René, 42, 53, 187
Picasso, Pablo, 17
Pièce, 123
Pierre Pathelin, 63
Pinero, Arthur Wing, 29, 195, 196
Pixerécourt, Guillaume de, 163
Plays
  full-length, 36–38
  one-act, 26, 175, 185, 188
  short, 26, 37, 42, 182, 183
Plots, use of, 30–31, 41, 66, 76, 97, 109
Poetic theater, 24, 31, 34, 191
  and poetic elements, 25
Pougy, Liane de, 14
Presle, Micheline, 84
Proust, Marcel, 12–13, 18
Psychological elements, 156, 172–73
Puce a l'oreille, La, 7, 28, 36, 37, 41, 45, 48, 56, 63, 71–73, 80, 81, 86, 142, 157–65, 166, 190

Quiproquo, use of, 7–8, 29, 30, 33, 38, 47–48, 76, 88, 96, 98, 107, 143, 153, 157, 159, 170, 178, 195

Racine, Jean, 197
Realism, elements of, 13, 16, 25, 38, 50–51, 53–54, 64, 68, 121, 131, 143, 163, 174, 195
Realism movement, 18, 52, 53
Réjane, 24
Religious satire, 141–42, 154
Renaissance theater, 25, 66
Renaud, Madeleine, 79, 83, 174
Repetition, use of, 44–45, 89
Ritchard, Cyril, 174
Romantic drama, 22, 24, 34, 163
Rostand, Edmond, 24, 25
Ruban, Le, 26, 56, 123
Ruy Blas (Hugo), 34

Sadomasochistic elements, 73, 159
Salle Luxembourg, 129–30
Salle Richelieu, 129
Salon comedies, 7
Sarcey, Francisque (quoted), 101
Sardou, Victorien, 22, 23, 52
Satire, use of, 65, 103, 108, 131, 140, 154, 155, 183–84
Scribe, Eugène, 22, 23, 25, 35, 40, 154, 163

Second Empire, 18, 24
Secret, device of, 28, 35–36, 162
Settings, 53–54, 98, 149
Shakespeare, William, 197
Shapiro, Norman R., 76, 193
Shaw, George Bernard, 23, 194
Short plays, 26, 37, 42, 182, 183
Situation comedy, 8, 20, 28, 29, 41–42, 44–45, 48–49, 65, 66, 74, 101, 111, 120, 132, 135, 195
Slapstick, 98, 114, 120
Social commentary, 25, 58, 65, 90, 98, 103, 108, 114, 121, 130, 154–55, 173
Stage directions, 32, 38–40, 54, 98, 115, 149, 157, 177, 193
Strindberg, August, 18, 67, 188
Structure of plays, 27, 120, 124, 132, 155
Sudermann, Hermann, 29
Surrealism, 149, 191
Symbolist movement, 18, 24–25
Système Ribadier, Le, 28, 46

Tailhade, Laurent, 12
Tailleur pour dames, 8, 24, 28, 45, 53, 55, 76–90
Tartuffe (Molière), 27

Tempo of plays, 27, 29–30, 34, 35, 37, 40, 74, 98, 101, 109, 120, 131, 141, 188, 196
Theater of the Absurd, 20, 50, 98–99, 149
Théâtre-Antoine, 65, 84
Théâtre complet, 166
Théâtre de l'Oeuvre, 24
Théâtre-Libre, 24, 52, 53, 64, 108
Themes, 8, 27, 91, 186
Thesis plays, 22, 70, 123–24, 154
13 Rue de l'Amour (Monsieur chasse), 9, 28, 57, 91–100
Tom Cobb (Gilbert), 195
Touchard, Pierre-Aimé, 129–30
Toulouse-Lautrec, 12
Tragedy, classical, 34–35, 197
Tragic elements, 27–28, 197
Translations of plays, 9–10, 157, 192–94
Twins, device of, 157
Tynan, Kenneth, 140, 174

Ubu roi (Jarry), 18, 25, 69
Universal Exposition, 17, 144

Uzès, Duchess of, 142

Valéry, Paul, 156
Vaudeville tradition, 7, 9, 22–23, 24, 29, 44, 47, 49–50, 52, 157, 195–96
and Feydeau, 19–20, 26, 27, 31, 48, 50–51, 68, 90, 91, 107, 115, 121, 130, 141, 145, 156, 163, 179–80, 189
Verneuil, Louis, 16
Violence, elements of, 8, 74, 90, 123, 164, 178, 196–97, 199
Vitaly, Georges, 81
Vlaminck, Maurice de, 17
Vultures, The (Becque), 66

Well-made play, 21–23, 24, 28, 33, 35, 38, 48, 113, 124, 143, 152–53, 154, 155, 162, 163
Whitehead, Paxton, 192
William II of Germany, 15
Woman of Paris (Becque), 66

Zola, Emile, 163